Making a
Difference

Rachel T. Hare-Mustin is Professor of Counseling and Human Relations at Villanova University in Pennsylvania and a clinical psychologist in private practice. Her scholarly work has focused on constructivism and gender theory in psychotherapy and family therapy. She has also written on ethics in psychology and carried out research on attitudes toward motherhood. She has received the Distinguished Publication Award of the Association for Women in Psychology. Among her recent publications is her chapter on the problem of gender in family therapy theory in *Women in Families*, edited by Monica McGoldrick, Carol Anderson, and Froma Walsh (New York: Norton, 1989).

Jeanne Marecek is Professor of Psychology and a member of the Women's Studies Program at Swarthmore College in Pennsylvania. Her scholarly work concerns critical studies of gender theory in psychology, and gender issues in mental health and psychotherapy. She has recently contributed chapters on gender and mental health to *Community Psychology*, edited by Margaret S. Gibbs, Juliana R. Lachenmeyer, and Janet Sigal (New York: Gardner, forthcoming) and *Women and Gender Roles* by Irene H. Frieze, Jacquelynne Eccles, Paula Johnson, Diane Ruble, and Gail Zellman (New York: Norton, forthcoming).

Bernice Lott is a Professor of Psychology and Women's Studies at the University of Rhode Island. She teaches social psychology at the undergraduate and graduate levels and has published in the areas of interpersonal attraction, sexist discrimination, and theoretical issues in feminist psychology. She has been honored twice by the Association for Women in Psychology with a Distinguished Publication Award and was named by her university in 1988 as the recipient of its Scholarly Excellence Award. Her most recent book is *Women's Lives: Themes and Variations in Gender Learning* (Monterey, CA: Brooks/Cole, 1987).

Jill G. Morawski is Associate Professor of Psychology at Wesleyan University, Middletown, Connecticut. Her contribution to this book is part of an ongoing exploration of postmodern theories of gender. She is interested in delineating the ways in which knowledge is organized, warranted, and shared and has completed various historical studies on this issue. She recently edited *The Rise of Experimentation in American Psychology* (New Haven: Yale University Press, 1988).

Rhoda Unger is Professor of Psychology and Director of the All-College Honors Program at Montclair State College in New Jersey. She has been interested in issues related to the methodology and epistemology of feminist psychology, as well as the social psychology of gender, for many years. She has received the Carolyn W. Sherif Award from the Division of the Psychology of Women of the American Psychological Association and the Distinguished Publication Award of the Association for Women in Psychology. Among her recent work is an edited book, *Representations: Social Constructions of Gender* (Amityville, NY: Baywood, 1989).

Making a Difference

Psychology and the Construction of Gender

EDITED BY

Rachel T. Hare-Mustin & Jeanne Marecek

Yale University Press   New Haven & London

Set in Trump type by
The Composing Room of Michigan, Inc.
Printed in the United States of America.

Library of Congress Cataloging-in-Publication Data
Making a difference: Psychology and the construction of gender / by Rachel T. Hare-Mustin . . . [et al.] ; edited by Rachel T. Hare-Mustin and Jeanne Marecek.
   p. cm.
  Includes bibliographical references.
  ISBN 0–300–04715–0 (alk. paper)
  1. Sex role. 2. Women—Psychology. I. Hare-Mustin, Rachel T.
  Marecek, Jeanne
HQ1075.M34 1990
305.3—dc20   89–38800
                                                CIP

The paper in this book meets the guidelines of permanence and durability of the Committee on Production Guidelines for Book Longevity of the Council on Library Resources.

10 9 8 7 6 5 4 3 2 1

To our mothers, who made the difference

Contents

Preface

In a period when what we know and how we know are once again challenging academic disciplines, feminist theorists have raised questions about our ways of knowing men and women. In psychology, feminists have challenged what we know about men and women, that is, the findings of conventional research. In this book we ask how we know about men and women and how psychology has contributed to the meaning of gender in the daily lives of men and women. Psychology had sought to separate from its forebear, philosophy, by identifying itself with natural science. We reexamine this identification in the light of contemporary challenges. In exploring these issues, we hope this book will involve readers in the ongoing conversations about feminist theory and postmodern approaches to psychology.

Both of us have been engaged with the issues of gender and meaning in relation to research and practice in psychology for nearly a decade. Some of our ideas have been presented at professional and scientific meetings, some have appeared in journal articles. An earlier version of chapter 2 appeared in the *American Psychologist*. Ensuing conversations with colleagues in psychology, in the therapeutic professions, and in women's studies have pushed us to clarify our ideas and stimulated us to think more deeply. As our ideas have evolved, our contributions to this book as editors and authors have been equal.

To further our own thinking and that of others about gender theory in psychology, we organized a symposium for the American Psychological Association meeting in August 1987 on "The Meaning of Gender." We invited three respected scholars in psychology, Bernice Lott, Jill Morawski, and Rhoda Unger, to join us. The enthusiasm for our presentations at the symposium encouraged us to proceed with this book.

The book opens with an introductory chapter that describes some of the ways in which psychology has dealt with women and the question of the difference between women and men. As psychologists, we are interested in the processes by which gender, like other social categories, is constructed. Psychology has long emphasized the study of individual differences. We present feminist challenges to this tradition.

Chapter 2, "Gender and the Meaning of Difference: Postmodernism and Psychology," by Rachel T. Hare-Mustin and Jeanne Marecek, describes more fully the debate on the meaning of difference and details the contributions that feminist psychology has made to it. We demonstrate how constructivism can be fruitfully applied to current representations of gender in psychology, particularly to representations of gender as difference. We suggest how the linguistic categories available in the culture, the modes of explanation privileged by the culture, and the dominant cultural ideology influence constructions of reality. Under conditions of social inequality, privileged members of society have control over meaning-making, and thus representations of reality serve the interests of those who authorize them. It is only when gender is disrupted as a category that its instability becomes apparent and other marginalized meanings emerge.

Chapter 3, "Dual Natures or Learned Behavior: The Challenge to Feminist Psychology," by Bernice Lott, points to the remarkable diversity in behavior associated with each gender. Psychologists have found considerable overlap in gender characteristics of men and women. Differences between them are less pervasive than has been popularly thought. Bernice Lott suggests that behavior does not depend on male or female sex but on acquired attitudes, expectations, sanctions, and the situational demands that separate the experiences of girls and boys, women and men. The social context and the human capacity for learning critically influence behaviors identified as masculine and feminine. She also addresses a major variable that distinguishes the adult lives of most women and men: power.

In Chapter 4, "Imperfect Reflections of Reality: Psychology Constructs Gender," Rhoda Unger challenges the idea of stable gender differences by pointing out the extent to which behaviors associated with gender vary according to specific social and interpersonal contexts. Rather than devising a taxonomy of ways in which men and women differ, Rhoda Unger thinks that social psychologists should focus on the social settings that create gendered behavior. This logic poses a sharp challenge to the traditional psychology experiment. If settings create behavior, then the laboratory experiment, which tries to remove the influence of the broader social setting, has limitations for the study of gender. More generally, Rhoda Unger examines several of the ways in which the traditional norms, assumptions, and practices of social psychology shape the study of gender. She counters with several innovations that would direct the study of gender into new and potentially more useful directions.

Chapter 5, "Toward the Unimagined: Feminism and Epistemology in Psychology," by Jill Morawski, suggests a future direction for feminist scholars concerned with transforming the structure of the psychology of gender. Jill Morawski notes that despite the tremendous intellectual accomplishments of feminists, there have been no fundamental changes in the way gender is conceptualized in psychology. Feminists have influenced psychological research, largely through the study of psychological androgyny, but androgyny research has reached an impasse. This impasse is rooted in the social relations constituting scientific work: the social marginality of women researchers, the way empiricist science curtails critical questioning and self-reflexiveness, and the reproduction of relations of power in science. The author offers an alternative epistemology for the future.

In our concluding chapter, "Beyond Difference," we observe that the politics of gender has become the politics of difference. We believe there is a need to reconstruct gender and we call for a paradigmatic shift beyond existing dualisms.

We draw inspiration from different sources for this book.

Rachel's interest in epistemology developed from early acquaintance with Gestalt perceptual theory, notably the ideas of Wolfgang Köhler, Hans Wallach, David Krech, Kurt Lewin, and Tolman's Sign-Gestalt learning theory. Edna Heidbreder served as a model through her work on systems in psychology and her cognitive studies. Rachel also recognizes the influence of systems and communication theorists such as Gregory Bateson and Paul Watzlawick, and colleagues concerned with theory in family therapy such as Salvador Minuchin and Jay Haley. Support and stimulation have also come from many friends in the forefront of family therapy, especially Monica McGoldrick, Marilyn Mason, Betty Carter, and Morris Taggart. Above all, Gilbert Mustin deserves thanks for his consistent encouragement of the project and faith in its accomplishment.

Jeanne traces much of her interest in epistemology and critical theory to work with colleagues in the women's studies programs at Swarthmore, the University of Wisconsin, and the University of Pennsylvania. Interdisciplinary teaching, first with Mary Poovey and then with Abbe Blum, was an important context for learning about poststructuralism and other postpositivist approaches. A sabbatical leave funded in part by a Eugene M. Lang Fellowship provided that most scarce commodity—time for uninterrupted work. In addition, Jeanne recognizes the support and challenges offered by her reading group on gender studies—Jeanne Allen, Joy Charlton, Michelle Fine, Carole Joffe, Louise Kidder, Demie Kurz, Joan Shapiro, and Ronnie Steinberg. Special thanks are due to Mary Crawford, Jon Copeland, Diane Kravetz, and Scott Gilbert for unfailing inspiration and encourgement.

                        Rachel T. Hare-Mustin   Jeanne Marecek

July 1989
Westport Point, Massachusetts

1

On Making a Difference

RACHEL T. HARE-MUSTIN AND JEANNE MARECEK

A difference that makes no difference is no difference.
Information is news about a difference.

From Aristotle's time to the present, Western knowledge has been organized around a series of dualities and dichotomies. In Western society we easily slide into a focus on differences and dualities when we organize the world about us. Psychology is part of this tradition based on operations of comparing and contrasting. But to see both sides of a problem is the surest way to prevent its solution because there are always more than two sides.

Difference does not exist in a vacuum. Our meanings derive from our interactions with the world and with one another. There is no world without words. But all communication is predicated on context, a pattern of relationships and connections. Gregory Bateson (1972) has pointed out that without context there is no meaning. Hence the assertion that a difference that makes no difference is no difference.

In Western thought male and female are often represented as a dichotomy and used as a metaphor to signify contrast, opposition, or complementarity. What do we make of gender differences? What do they mean? Why are there so many? Why are there so few? Perhaps we should be asking: What is the point of differences? What lies beyond difference? Difference aside, what else is gender? The overarching question is about the choice of question.

We find ourselves in a moment of epistemological change, at the twilight of the Newtonian era of naive empiricism. The hallmark of this era has been the belief that the human observer, no longer enmeshed in space and time, can stand apart from the world that he or she observes. Attempts to achieve this stance, epitomized by the scientific method, have led to significant accomplishments reflected in changes in knowledge and daily life. Now we are entering a period of indeterminacy, marked by Einstein's theory of relativity, the Heisenberg principle, and chaos theory. The opposition of observer and observed can no longer be sustained. We now can acknowledge that the observer is never wholly separate from the thing observed. As Einstein noted, our theories determine what we can observe.

Psychologists interested in gender have carried out many empirical studies of gender differences and gender roles during the past fifteen years. Through their work, gender has emerged as a significant category of social reality. But to date little attention has been given to the diverse ways in which gender has been represented in psychological theory. This has hindered conceptual progress. Depending on how gender is construed—as a structural principle of social relations between males and females, as culture-specific behavioral attributes of individuals, as essential male and female nature—varied questions arise, varied modes of inquiry are developed, and varied approaches to personal and sociopolitical change are demanded.

All meanings are products of human interaction. Consequently, meaning is neither static nor singular. Meanings are multiple, changing, and always being renegotiated and regenerated by communication and action. Language is the key to meaning because all explanations, all theories, occur within language.

But neither description nor explanation is the same as experience itself. When we describe prior experience, our descriptions slide into narrative. The traditional narrative structures of temporal ordering and of logical cause and effect transform the chaotic nature of experience. Explanation, similarly, is not a mirror of the world but an assortment of pictures of the world that we create to connect one experience with another. Ultimately, our ideas about things, which are our theories, reveal our value systems—how we view the world.

The meanings of gender are also multiple and shifting. In this book we examine meanings of gender, especially those meanings that have figured prominently in psychological theory and research. By joining critical debate on the construction of gender, our purpose is to expand the psychological study of gender from empiricist fact-finding to a scrutiny of meaning-making and knowledge as social relations.

Making a Difference

The dual meaning of the title of this book, "Making a Difference," reveals two central premises of our work. First, differences between women and men, by and large, are made; that is, gender is not a natural category based on essential differences between the sexes. Some consider biology to produce immutable sex differences, but both in an individual lifetime and from a broader historical perspective, biological differences are not immutable. The environment modifies biology, nurture influences nature. Even menstruation may be a feature of modern life rather than a biological universal. For women like !Kung women who experience early marriage, repeated pregnancies, and a short life span, menstruation as a regular monthly event is rare. In addition, when women are poorly nourished or physically active and have a relatively low proportion of body fat, they typically do not ovulate regularly and thus do not menstruate.

Culture and technology can render "immutable" differences irrelevant. With mechanization, differences between women and men in physical size and muscular strength have become less relevant to occupational success. With the computer revolution, differences in cognitive capacities and such skills as memory, rote calculation, translation, and spelling are similarly becoming less relevant.

Even reproductive capacities that were thought to be the bedrock of sexual difference have diminished in their importance as a result of such technological innovations as contraception, surrogate motherhood, bottle feeding, artificial insemination by donor, and in vitro fertilization. Although only women can give birth and lactate, it is a cultural choice, not a biological imperative, that assigns the responsibility for raising children to them. In any case, reproductive specialization is only a limited part of our highly evolved modern life and is salient for only a portion of the life span, which extends for many years beyond the species' reproductive activity.

Gender is an invention of human societies, a feat of imagination and industry. This feat is multifaceted. One facet involves laborious efforts to transform male and female children into masculine and feminine adults. We call this rearing children or educating them. Another facet involves creating and maintaining the social arrangements that sustain differences in men's and women's consciousness and behavior, such as the demands of office and kitchen. Through these arrangements, gender symbolism is supported by the division of labor of men and women. A third facet involves meaning: creating the linguistic and conceptual structures that shape and discipline our imagination of male and female, as well as creating the meaning of gender itself. Thus, gender is a way of organizing everyday life.

"Making a Difference" has a second meaning. How we define gender difference—what we take gender to mean—makes a difference. Debates about gender are not merely exercises carried out in the halls and laboratories of academe and duly reported in textbooks and professional journals; rather, the outcome of such debates has a broad range of consequences. What we make of gender and how we define male and female have an influence on how people see themselves and the world. The meaning of gender also has an influence on behavior, social arrangements, and the organization of such crucial social institutions as work, reproduction, child care, education, and the family. For this reason debates about gender have achieved prominence in the popular media as well as in the scholarly press. These debates have involved political figures, the judiciary, the clergy, and other representatives of the major institutions of society.

In modern Western societies, psychology and the social sciences more generally are accorded an important role in defining normative behaviors and acceptable social practices. Psychologists are given authority to prescribe certain behaviors and practices and to sanction others. Their authority rests on two related attributes. First, psychologists are viewed as experts whose methods of inquiry are believed to yield a truthful and accurate account of social reality. Second, scientific pronouncements are held to be free from the contaminating influences of the scientist's self-interest and personal values. Psychologists' prescriptions for behaviors, social relations, or courses of action have been accepted as value-free standards of health or maturity rather than as standards reflecting particular moral or ethical values.

But now, scholars from within the social sciences as well as others are raising increasingly trenchant objections to these claims of expertise and impartiality. Efforts are being made to recast the relationship between psychology and society. As a cultural institution, psychology is of course continuous with society; it does not and cannot stand apart from it. It shares the assumptions and meanings of the larger society. Critics have pointed out that the study of human behavior by psychologists and other social scientists has too often served to reconfirm the status quo and to reify existing social reality. Seen from a contemporary vantage point, earlier prescriptions for female behavior and gender relations offer striking evidence for this; for example, psychologists at the turn of the century asserted that higher education might develop women's brains, but that this would cause their ovaries to shrink so that they would be incapable of bearing children. Psychologists of the post-World War II era condemned mothers' employment outside the home as dangerous to children's moral and social development. Only now are we coming to recognize the social, historical, and political particularity of psychology.

This book explores the issues of making a difference and psychology's construction of gender from a number of vantage points. As psychologists, we are interested in the processes by which gender, like other categories of social reality, is constructed and given meaning through social interactions. We are especially interested in the construction of gender in the discourse of psychologists: in their experiments, their theories, their writings, and their psychotherapy practices. In these essays, we consider the arguments, language, and symbols that psychologists use both in their communications with one another and in their communications to those outside the profession, such as students and therapy clients, as well as the public at large.

Psychology Discovers Women: The First Half-Century

Gender theory in present-day psychology draws on developments in psychology and in feminist thought. The varied approaches to studying gender reflect the diversity and fragmentation of the discipline of psychology as a whole, a diversity and fragmentation that are increasing rather than abating as the discipline matures (Bronfenbrenner, Kessel, Kessen & White, 1986). Before turning to the examination of gender theory in psychology, we shall review briefly how the study of women in psychology has proceeded.

In much of traditional psychology, women, whether as investigators or as objects of inquiry, were more or less absent. There were few female psychologists, and women's experiences were regarded as too unimportant to be a focus of inquiry. One could call this "womanless" psychology (Crawford & Marecek, 1989).

Traditional psychology was womanless in a number of ways. Women were underrepresented as the objects of inquiry. White male college sophomores in introductory psychology courses were the typical participants in psychological studies. The results of studies of male subjects were often generalized to formulate universal laws of *human* (that is, male *and* female) behavior. Men's experiences were more visible to psychologists in part because of the salience of the public sphere, including paid work, military life, and civic activities, where men predominate.

Concepts in psychology were defined from the point of view of male experience. The Oedipus complex, for example, which refers to psychological processes of male development, was held to be a central developmental experience for both sexes. The concept of penis envy assumed that the penis held the same primacy and significance for girls as for boys. These explanatory constructs can be seen as metaphors derived from male experience. Other psychological concepts, seemingly more gender-neutral, also were defined from the point of view of male experience: ego, self, dependency, and intelligence.

Traditional psychology was virtually womanless in another regard as well. There were relatively few women participating in the discipline. Those few were often rendered invisible or marginal, deprived of recognition for their work, or denied the resources needed for productive scholarship. Even those with notable names were invisible. Thus Freud implies Sigmund, not Anna; Sherif implies Muzafer, not Carolyn. The Masculinity and Femininity Scales of Lewis Terman and Carolyn Miles are known as Terman's; the Thematic Apperception Test developed by Henry Murray and Christiana Morgan is referred to as Murray's TAT. In a recent interview Erik Erikson and Joan Erikson revealed that their work on the life-cycle theory was done jointly (Goleman, 1988); however, only his name appears as author.

One remedy for the invisibility of women in psychology has been to refocus attention on the contributions and achievements of exceptional women. This is an important advance, but only a partial one, since it does not effectively challenge the male norm of womanless psychology. Only great women—Anna Freud and Karen Horney, for example—are accorded a place alongside Pavlov and Skinner. But according recognition to the few exceptional women in psychology does not change the fact that males continue to shape the discipline and control the research agenda. For the most part, the small number of exceptional women went unremarked. This can be seen as a reflection of the cultural belief in the survival of the fittest: Everyone has an equal chance at success; those with the necessary capabilities succeed, the rest are simply "not good enough." For feminists, however, the scarcity of women whose contributions are recognized as exceptional raises the question of what obstacles were placed before other women to prevent them from similar accomplishment and recognition.

Individual Differences

It is often said that the individual has become the central organizing principle of American culture, replacing the idea of God, which was supreme in Western societies in the Middle Ages. A dominant theme of American society has been that of independence, privatization, individualism, and personal control. Psychology has helped shape and support ideas of the individual as a self-contained, even noble entity.

The individual-centered view can lead to elevating individual actions as determinants. The influence of the context in which action takes place is downplayed. However, knowing only the behavioral setting, such as church or post office, can lead to more accurate predictions of behavior than knowing an individual's sex, race, or class. It is said that behavior tends to engulf the field, capturing attention and obliterating the surrounding situation of which it is a part.

Further, proponents of the individual-centered view hold that maintaining sharp demarcations between persons is essential to good mental health and social functioning. Thus, independence, autonomy, and firm ego boundaries are goals of development. The task of understanding social systems and describing the social organization and interaction of groups, families, tribes, and aggregates has received far less attention in psychology.

Psychology has had a long tradition of focusing on individual differences. One of the major differences it has focused on has been the difference between men and women. The question of sex differences in individuals' interests, personality attributes, traits, and abilities emerges periodically as a focus of study; indeed, the question of sex differences seems most likely to garner psychologists' attention whenever public controversy over women's roles erupts—that is, when women demand to be accorded privileges and opportunities similar to those of men. Psychological research on sex differences aims to ascertain the ways in which men and women differ, not the ways in which they are similar. This focus on individual differences by psychologists has supported the social status quo.

Historically, the differences between men and women were usually attributed to essential biological factors. When differences between men and women are attributed to biology, such differences come to be seen as universal and natural, if not morally correct (Krull, 1989). Moreover, biological determinism, like divine right in earlier times, serves as a justification for social inequities. Darwinian ideas of evolutionary biology, which regard woman as a man whose evolution has been arrested, have persisted into the current era. Women are seen as tied down by their biological nature, and men as having achieved rationality and free will. Biological differences have served to contain women in terms of what women's place *must* be. Women's behavior was often seen as a function of their biological nature, whereas men's moods and behavior were rarely attributed to their biological nature (Shields, 1975). As recently as the 1960s, a woman's "raging hormones" were held to make her unstable and therefore unfit to hold high political office. (Congresswoman Patsy Mink purportedly answered this charge by asking her male critic, "What's your excuse?")

Even today, women's moods are often ascribed to the hormonal changes of the menstrual cycle. A fascinating case study in the cultural construction of illness is the invention of PMS (premenstrual syndrome) by the medical and psychiatric establishment (Parlee, 1989). The fact that a small number of women experience severe difficulties associated with menstruation is used as the basis for diagnosing many woman who experience minor discomfort as having PMS and prescribing medication for them. Further, the widely held assumption that menopause is associated with depression has not held up under close scrutiny. Using epidemiological data, Lenore Radloff (1980) found that depression was no more common at menopause than at other times in a woman's life. Other researchers have reported that many women experience increased satisfaction and higher self-esteem at this life stage (Baruch, Barnett & Rivers, 1983). Moreover, the notion that the biological processes of pregnancy, childbirth, and lactation release certain "maternal instincts" is still put forth despite the lack of systematic evidence (Badinter, 1981; Braverman, 1989). Evolved intelligence, not instinct, is what is used to help infants survive (Humphrey, 1976). The cultural constructions of gender have emphasized hormones and biological processes as determinants of women's behavior and feelings but not of men's.

Gender, as opposed to sex, was rarely a category of analysis in traditional psychology. Little attention was paid to the cultural elaboration of sex-typed characteristics or to the patterns of norms and sanctions by which society regulated the behavior of males and females; for example, psychologists did not concern themselves with the early stereotyping experiences of children in school. Only in the past few decades have questions been raised about the channeling of girls into arts and boys into science, the exclusion of girls from sports and competitive activities, and the use of curricular materials that omitted the experiences of girls and women. Only recently have psychologists recognized the significant influence of separate spaces and social barriers on the behavior of women and men.

The history of psychology also reveals a consistent view of women as Other, as different from and inferior to men. Women were seen as the repository of nonmasculine traits, of an "otherness." This view can be seen in the theories of Freud and other early psychodynamic theorists. Psychotherapy originally was concerned almost exclusively with women patients, and it probably never would have survived without the pervasive unhappiness of many women. In spite of this, misogynist practices and sexist assumptions in therapy prevailed; for example, classic psychoanalytic theory regarded women as having weak superegos, low sex drives, a diminished sense of self-worth, and so on. In her satiric review of sex research, Margot Sims (1982) highlights this bias by pointing out how women could have been made to appear superior if theorists had chosen to focus on factors favoring females, such as organ specialization, correlation of libido and climacteric, and fetal death rates.

A similar pattern of bias is evident in psychologists' research on individual differences. Throughout much of the history of the discipline, psychologists readily imputed difference and deficiency to individuals from so-called inferior social categories: racial and ethnic minorities, recent immigrants, and the lower socioeconomic classes. The fact that academic psychologists by and large were white males from elite social backgrounds probably contributed to their readiness to see difference and to attribute deficiency to those unlike themselves (Sherwood & Nataupsky, 1968).

Feminist Critiques of Difference Research

Feminist psychologists have questioned the study of male-female differences in psychology. Their work has taken two important directions, each of which has raised doubts about previously accepted conclusions. First, they have challenged the content of much traditional research on male-female difference and pointed to the failure to replicate patterns of differences. A recent review of research on sex differences in cognitive abilities, for example, shows that such differences appear to have declined precipitously over the past two decades (Feingold, 1988). Likewise, recent studies of presumed differences in personality traits and social behaviors cast doubt on previous findings. As some social psychologists have pointed out, the *perception* of differences between men and women has been far greater than findings on the differences themselves.

A second major product of feminist efforts has been a wide-ranging critique of methods of studying male-female differences. As Carol Jacklin (1981) has noted, the more carefully a study is carried out, the less likely it is that sex differences will emerge. Among the flaws she has identified as prevalent are inadequate conceptualizations of the term *difference*, failure to distinguish the statistical significance of a difference from the size of a difference, the assumption that all sex-related differences are a result of genetic or innate differences, and a disregard for differences in how men and women report their experiences. For example, Pepper Schwartz [1987] found that men who "helped at home" reported spending three to four hours a day washing dishes, an amount any housewife would regard as incredible.

One of the most common methodological errors is the confusion of within-sex differences with between-sex differences (Jacklin, 1981). Within-sex differences are differences among members of one sex. Between-sex differences are differences between women and men. One example of confusing the two is the practice of studying only one sex and then claiming how the other sex might differ if studied by the same approach. One study often cited as evidence of gender differences in moral reasoning looked at women making decisions about whether or not to terminate a pregnancy. Not only were no men studied, but there is no comparable moral dilemma for men. Another study attempted to identify uniquely "womanly" ways of knowing through a study of women's intellectual styles; the study did not include a comparison group of men.

Carol Jacklin's critique of conceptual and methodological flaws in traditional sex-difference research also offers an account of adequate methods of study and analysis. Critics of traditional studies of sex differences often suggest more use of exploratory studies and pretests, more careful selection of subjects to be sampled, better measuring techniques, and more careful choice of statistical tests. But the vast and growing catalogue of ways in which an investigator's stance influences procedures, observations, and interpretations leads us to doubt that research in psychology and the other social sciences can be perfected even by efforts made in good faith.

Feminist research on male-female differences has challenged orthodox psychology's construction of sex and gender. Many of the sex differences that had been put forward by traditional psychology were shown to be founded on shaky empirical bases, could not be replicated, or reflected the effects of cultural conditioning rather than biological nature. The results of feminist research on male-female difference also furnish a valuable resource for political activism directed at gaining equality for women. If women are as capable as men and similar in traits, temperaments, and motivations, then it is difficult to justify unequal access to education, barriers to equal employment, and discriminatory legal statutes.

Feminist research on sex differences has its drawbacks as well.

Whether and how men and women differ is a question received from traditional psychology, and the research program is reactive rather than proactive. The energies of feminists are deflected from questions of their own choosing in order to counter exaggerated claims of difference, refute claims of female deficiency, and oppose policies and practices based on those claims. Moreover, continued attention to debates on gender difference heightens the importance of those debates. By joining the debate on "female nature" and "women's place," feminists inadvertently lend credence to that debate.

Gender Roles and Gender-Role Socialization

As long as male behavior remains the standard in the culture, women's differences from men will be regarded as deficiencies. It follows from this that to be considered the equal of men, women must be "equal to" or "as good as" men. Inevitably, much work in feminist psychology reflects this cultural assumption in one way or another. The study of cultural conditioning and gender-role socialization, for example, investigates how behaviors and attitudes deemed appropriate for each gender are learned and maintained. Much of the work on socialization has investigated women's supposed deficiencies and shortcomings: fear of success, learned helplessness, math anxiety, lack of leadership qualities, and low self-esteem. Studies of gender and psychopathology also reflect cultural assumptions. Feminine gender-role socialization is regarded as the cause of psychological disorders prevalent among women, including agoraphobia, depression, and anorexia nervosa (Hare-Mustin, 1983; Marecek, in press). Other examples can be seen in many of the self-help books and "pop psychology" guides for women in which the point of view is put forth that because of their feminine socialization (or their lack of masculine socialization), women are or have a problem (Worell, 1988).

The emphasis on gender-role socialization has a number of positive features. It shifts attention from biological differences between men and women to the effects of cultural conditioning and stereotyping. Gender roles, gender stereotypes, and socialization are seen as processes that account for many of the observed differences between women and men, including differences in behavior, interests, and traits.

The roles of wife and mother have received special attention and analysis by feminists. The effects of training all women for marriage and motherhood, regardless of their individual interests and potential, have been a paramount concern. The family was identified as the primary beneficiary and locus of women's labor as well as a primary source of identity for most women. In spite of this identification, little emphasis was placed on how women's needs could be met in families. Even many feminists focus on mothering largely in terms of the needs of the child. Rather than ask husbands and children to change, women have been encouraged to meet their needs for achievement and support outside the family, for example, in friendships with other women and in the workplace. Seldom was the assignment of housework exclusively to women challenged, even though its repetitive and unappreciated routines were found by researchers to be associated with women's depression (Hare-Mustin, 1987).

Femininity—and to a lesser extent, masculinity—has also received attention and analysis. Femininity was identified with passivity, nurturance, adornment, and virtue, whereas masculinity has been identified with agonistic activity, ritualistic combat, overt sexuality, and possessive individualism. From Homer's time until today, the first requirement of heroism was the exclusion of women as participants. Such social critics as Irving Howe have pointed out that masculine roles and stereotypes have supported the politics of macho swagger and possessive individualism. Occasionally psychologists have considered the cultural conditioning and socialization experiences that give rise to masculinity in men. Psychologists, however, have been far less interested in the detrimental effects of male socialization than female socialization. Similarly, there has been limited interest on the part of therapists in helping men break out of stereotyped roles or overcome their masculinity.

The concept of gender-role socialization has been a powerful and useful explanatory device. It enabled feminist psychologists to highlight certain aspects of experience; nonetheless, it obscured others. Much of the work pertaining to gender-role socialization fits within the broad framework of social learning theory. Social learning theory seeks to explain how people come to behave in accord with the rewards and punishments present in their environments. Like behaviorism, its parent theory, social learning theory is pragmatic and focused on the present and future. It is concerned with how behavior is learned and sustained at the micro level. It is not concerned with the broad origins of gendered behavior in a historical and sociopolitical context, but rather with contingent behaviors in closely defined situations. Uncritical adoption of the social learning paradigm allows the researcher to evade some crucial questions: What are the ultimate origins of gender roles? How can male dominance and female subordination be explained? Is dominance merely a set of skills that women have not had the opportunity to learn?

Another drawback of the psychology of gender roles is that thus far it has obscured the diversity of women's lives by implying that all women are subject to the same socialization pressures and respond to these pressures in the same way. This is far from what has been observed. Gender roles are not totalizing. Rather, women from different ethnic groups, social classes, age cohorts, and possibly even geographic regions experience different pressures and resist or accede to them in different ways.

The focus on gender roles as constricting men's and women's opportunities and blocking self-expression ignores the fact that not all individuals find prescribed roles oppressive or confining.

Further, the single-minded focus on gender as a social category diverts attention from other categories, such as age, race, and class. Even these distinctions give way to others in some societies; for example, in China the predominant difference is not between male and female but between insider and outsider—between clan members and others or between Han Chinese and foreigners. Although gender is a predominant category of social life in our society, it is obviously not the sole category.

Not all situations are gendered. Under certain conditions men and women are expected to behave similarly. Moreover, the roles and behaviors associated with gender are always modulated by other influences; for example, the strictures regarding purdah and the seclusion of women in orthodox Muslim societies break down in the lowest social classes, where the survival of the household requires that women engage in market activities.

The emphasis on gender roles also obscures the commonalities between women and men. The masculine ideal of autonomy, for example, may be out of reach for women, but it may be unattainable for men as well. The exclusive focus on nurturance also may not be good for women either, because it overlooks the human need to receive care as well as to give it (Hare-Mustin & Marecek, 1986). As we discuss below, the construction of gender difference as restrictive definitions of male and female behavior ignores the fact that male roles and female roles are not equal or equally detrimental. Men's roles are associated with greater power and privilege, as well as greater social value, than women's roles.

The focus on roles and role conditioning can depoliticize the issue of gender. When gender is framed as roles and role conditioning, the issue of inequality recedes since gender roles appear complementary, that is, equal and opposite. This can explain why the concepts of gender roles and role conditioning have gained broad appeal in the discipline of psychology and in the popular media as well (Mednick, 1989).

The Other Side of Difference

Another feminist approach to the study of women and gender focuses on the many ways that women's experience *does* differ from men's. Rather than looking for ways to dissolve those differences, some theorists call for a positive reevaluation of those differences. They celebrate the personal and cultural value of feminine qualities and of the female experience. These analyses have been simultaneously labeled as the most radical of feminist ideologies and as the most conservative and reactionary.

As chapter 2 discusses, there is both a radical and a reactionary potential in celebrating female difference. What is potentially radical is the challenge to the hierarchies embedded in conventional dichotomies of male-female, reason-emotion, culture-nature, good-bad, higher-lower. The emphasis on difference and the celebration of feminine qualities has a reactionary potential as well. The bifurcation of human qualities as masculine and feminine closely resembles conventional Western stereotypes. It invites differential treatment of the two sexes, as well as restricted access to certain roles, statuses, and opportunities on the basis of gender. Moreover, the emphasis on male-female difference easily leads to a false universalization, glossing over the many differences among members of each sex. Also, the emphasis on psychological difference centers attention on the personal and the individual, moving it away from the larger sociopolitical community.

The Future of Difference

The debate on difference has become an arena of struggle for feminist scholars in many disciplines. Although most of the arguments in the debate draw on psychological theories, and although the debate is fundamentally about the psychology of gender, psychologists themselves have not played a key role in the debate. In the essays that follow, we offer four psychological perspectives on the debate about difference. In doing so, our goal is to bring developments in feminist psychology to the feminist community at large and to invite others to join the conversation on difference.

In this book, we address how gender might be construed and studied, drawing on the past two decades of scholarship in feminist psychology. While acknowledging a debt to that work, we propose a redirection of attention toward new questions and new conceptualizations. Constructivism is explored as an alternative epistemology that can direct energy into new and potentially valuable forms of inquiry. A more self-reflexive approach to the psychology of gender is called for, with attention paid to the critical analysis of the established categories of psychological discourse. We also connect epistemological issues in feminist psychology with feminist thought in other disciplines, such as philosophy of science, sociology, and political theory.

In developing this book we have kept before us the words of one pundit who remarked, "If they can get you to ask the wrong question, they don't have to worry about your answer." In challenging the idea of gender difference, this book goes beyond the questions of traditional psychology, which have provided traditional answers, to try to move outside the categories in which psychologists customarily think. We show how the representation of gender on a continuum of difference has simplified and purified the concept of gender, obscuring the complexity of human action. As we point out in Chapter 6, a false symmetry has been created by the idea of difference, which has shielded both men and women from the discomforting recognition of inequality. We suggest new ways of viewing gender. Disrupting the seemingly fixed language of established meaning opens possibilities for moving beyond the question of difference.

REFERENCES

Badinter, E. (1981). *Mother love: Myth and reality.* New York: Macmillan.

Baruch, G., Barnett, R. & Rivers, C. (1983). *Lifeprints: New patterns of love and work for today's women.* New York: New American Library.

Bateson, G. (1972). *Steps to an ecology of mind.* New York: Ballantine.

Braverman, L. (1989). Beyond the myth of motherhood. In M. McGoldrick, C. M. Anderson, & F. Walsh (Eds.), *Women in families: A framework for family therapy* (227–43). New York: Norton.

Bronfenbrenner, U., Kessel, F., Kessen, W. & White, S. (1986). Toward a critical social history of developmental psychology: A propaedeutic discussion. *American Psychologist, 41,* 1218–30.

Crawford, M. & Marecek, J. (1989). Psychology reconstructs the female: 1968–1988. *Psychology of Women Quarterly, 13,* 147–65.

Feingold, A. (1988). Cognitive gender differences are disappearing. *American Psychologist, 43,* 95–103.

Goleman, D. (1988, June 14). Erikson, in his own old age, expands his view of life. *New York Times,* C1, C14.

Hare-Mustin, R. T. (1983). An appraisal of the relationship of women and psychotherapy: 80 years after the case of Dora. *American Psychologist, 38,* 593–601.

Hare-Mustin, R. T. (1987). The problem of gender in family therapy theory. *Family Process, 26,* 15–27.

Hare-Mustin, R. T. & Marecek, J. (1986). Autonomy and gender: Some questions for therapists. *Psychotherapy, 23,* 205–12.

Humphrey, N. K. (1976). The social function of intellect. In P. P. G. Bateson & R. A. Hinde (Eds.), *Growing points in ethnology* (303–17). Cambridge: Cambridge University Press.

Jacklin, C. N. (1981). Methodological issues in the study of sex-related differences. *Developmental Review, 1,* 266–73.

Krull, M. (1989). Systemic thinking and ethics: Political implications of the systemic perspective. In J. Hargens (Ed.), *Systemic therapy: A European Perspective* (134–41). Broadstairs, Kent, U.K.: Borgmann.

Marecek, J. (in press). Psychological disorders of women. In I. H. Frieze, J. Eccles, D. Ruble, P. Johnson & G. Zellman (Eds.), *Women and gender roles.* New York: Norton.

Mednick, M. T. (1989). On the politics of psychological constructs: Stop the bandwagon, I want to get off. *American Psychologist, 44,* 1118–23.

Parlee, M. B. (1989, March). *The science and politics of PMS research.*

Invited address presented at the meeting of the Association for Women in Psychology, Newport, RI.

Radloff, L. S. (1980). Depression and the empty nest. *Sex Roles, 6,* 775–81.

Schwartz, P. (1987, June) *American couples: The intimate struggle for power.* Paper presented at the meeting of the American Family Therapy Association, Chicago, IL.

Sherwood, J. J. & Nataupsky, M. (1968). Predicting the conclusions of Negro-White intelligence research from the biographical characteristics of the investigator. *Journal of Personality and Social Psychology, 8,* 53–58.

Shields, S. A. (1975). Functionalism, Darwinism, and the psychology of women: A study in social myth. *American Psychologist, 30,* 739–54.

Sims, M. (1982). *On the necessity of bestializing the human female.* Boston, MA: South End Press.

Worell, J. (1988). Women's satisfaction in close relationships. *Clinical Psychology Review, 8,* 477–98.

2

Gender and the Meaning
of Difference

Postmodernism and Psychology

RACHEL T. HARE-MUSTIN AND JEANNE MARECEK

Conventional meanings of gender typically focus on difference, emphasizing how women differ from men. These differences have furnished support for the norm of male superiority. Until recently, psychological inquiry into gender has held to the construction of gender as difference. Thus, psychologists have focused on documenting differences between men and women, and their findings have served as scientific justification for male-female inequality (Lott, 1985; Morawski, 1985; Shields, 1975; Weisstein, 1971). When we examine theories of psychotherapy, we find that they, too, have supported the cultural meanings of gender (Hare-Mustin, 1983).

One recent line of inquiry by feminist psychologists has involved reexamining gender with the goal of deemphasizing difference by sorting out genuine male-female differences from stereotypes. Some examples include Janet Hyde's (1981) meta-analyses of cognitive differences, Eleanor Maccoby and Carolyn Jacklin's (1975) review of sex differences, and Jacquelynne Eccles's work on math achievement (Eccles, 1989; Eccles & Jacobs, 1986). The results of this work dispute the contention that many male-female differences are universal, dramatic, or enduring (Deaux, 1984; Unger, 1979; Wallston, 1981). Moreover, this line of inquiry sees the origins of difference as largely social and cultural rather than biological. Thus, most differences between males and females are seen as culturally specific and historically fluid.

Another line of inquiry, exemplified in recent feminist psychodynamic theories (e.g., Chodorow, 1978; Eichenbaum & Orbach, 1983; Miller, 1986), takes as its goal the reaffirmation of gender differences. Although these theories provide varying accounts of the origins of difference, they all emphasize deep-seated and enduring differences between women and men in what is referred to as core self-structure, identity, and relational capacities. Other theorists have extended this work to suggest that these gender differences in psychic structure give rise to cognitive differences, such as differences in moral reasoning and in acquiring and organizing knowledge (cf. Belenky, Clinchy, Goldberger & Tarule, 1986; Gilligan, 1982; Keller, 1985). These theories represent differences between men and women as essential, universal (at least within contemporary Western culture), highly dichotomized, and enduring.

These two lines of inquiry have led to two widely held but incompatible representations of gender: one that sees considerable similarity between males and females, and another that sees profound differences. Both groups of theorists have offered empirical evidence, primarily quantitative in the first case and qualitative in the second. We believe that it is unlikely that further empirical evidence will resolve the question of whether men and women are similar or different. The two lines of inquiry described here emerge from different intellectual traditions, construe their domains of study differently, and rely on such different methods that consensus on a given set of conclusions seems unlikely. Moreover, even if consensus were possible, the question of what constitutes differentness would remain.

What constitutes differentness is a vexing question for psychologists who study sex and gender. Research that focuses on average differences between men and women may produce one conclusion while research that focuses on the full range of variations and the overlap (or lack of overlap) at the extremes of the range may produce another (Luria, 1986). An illustration can make this clearer: Although on average, American men are several inches taller than American women, we can readily think of some men who are shorter than many or even most women. The size and direction of gender differences in social behaviors, such as aggression or helping, often vary according to the norms and expectations for men and women that are made salient by the setting in which the behavior takes place (Eagly & Crowley, 1986; Eagly & Steffen, 1986). Studies in experimental laboratories can produce different results from field observations in real settings. Even more troubling, the very criteria for deciding what should constitute a difference as opposed to a similarity are disputed. How much difference makes a difference? Even the anatomical differences between men and women seem trivial when humans are compared to daffodils or ducks.

What are we to make of the difference versus no difference debate? Rather than debating which of these representations of gender is "true," we shift to the metaperspective provided by postmodernism. From this perspective, we can entertain new and possibly more fruitful questions about representations of gender, including the political and social functions that the difference and no difference positions serve. This perspective opens the way to alternative representations of gender that would raise new questions or recast old ones for psychologists.

Postmodernism and Meaning

Two recent intellectual movements, constructivism and deconstruction, challenge the idea of a single meaning of reality and a single truth. Rather than concerning themselves with a search for "the truth," they inquire instead about the way meanings are negotiated, the control over meanings by those in authority, and how meanings are represented in language. The current interest in constructivism and deconstruction reflects the growing skepticism about the positivist tradition in science and essentialist theories of truth and meaning (Rorty, 1979). Both constructivism and deconstruction challenge these positions, asserting that the social context shapes knowledge, and that meanings are historically situated and constructed and reconstructed through the medium of language.

The connection between meaning and power has been a focus of postmodernist thinkers (Foucault, 1973; Jameson, 1981). Their inquiry into meaning focuses especially on language as the medium of cognitive life and communication. Language is seen not simply as a mirror of reality or a neutral tool (Taggart, 1985; Wittgenstein, 1960; 1967). As Bruner (1986) points out, language "imposes a point of view not only about the world to which it refers but toward the use of the mind in respect to this world" (121). Language highlights certain features of the objects it represents, certain meanings of the situations it describes. "The word—no matter how experimental or tentative or metaphoric—tends to replace the things being described" (Spence, 1987, 3). Once designations in language become accepted, one is constrained by them not only in communicating ideas to others, but in the generation of ideas as well (Bloom, 1981). Language inevitably structures one's own experience of reality as well as the experience of those to whom one communicates. Just as in any interaction we cannot "not communicate," so at some level we are always influencing one another and ourselves through language.

Meaning-making and control over language are important resources held by those in power. Like other valuable resources, they are not distributed equitably across the social hierarchy. Indeed, Barthes (1972) has called language a sign system used by the powerful to label, define, and rank. Language is never innocent. Throughout history, dominant groups have asserted their authority over language. Our purpose here is to draw attention to the fact that men's influence over language is greater than that of women; we do not argue that women have had no influence over language. Within most social groups, males have had privileged access to education and thus have had higher rates of literacy than females; this remains true in many developing countries today (Newland, 1979). Men's dominance in academic institutions influences the social production of knowledge, including the concepts and terms in which people think about the world (Andersen, 1983). In addition, more men are published and men control the print and electronic media (Strainchamps, 1974). The arbiters of language usage are primarily men, from Samuel Johnson and Noah Webster to H. L. Mencken and Strunk and White.

When meaning-making through language is concentrated among certain groups in society, the meanings put forth can only be partial, because they exclude the experiences of other social groups. Yet the dominant group's influence over meaning-making is such that partial meanings are represented as if they were complete. In the instance of male control over language, the use of the generic masculine is a ready example of representing a partial object, the masculine, as complete, that is, as encompassing both male and female. Although not all men have influence over language, for those who do, such authority confers the power to create the world from their point of view, in the image of their desires.

In this chapter, we try to rethink the psychology of gender from the vantage point of constructivism and deconstruction. We first take up constructivism. We examine various constructions of gender and identify the problems associated with the predominant meaning of gender, that of male-female difference. We then turn to deconstruction. We show how a deconstructive approach can reveal alternative meanings associated with gender. In therapy, deconstruction can be a means of disrupting clients' understanding of reality by revealing alternative meanings. New meanings offer new possibilities for action and thus can foster change. We do not provide an exhaustive review of sex differences in psychology or propose a new theory of gender. Rather, we shift the discussion to a metatheoretical level in order to consider gender theorizing. Our purpose is not to answer the question of what is the meaning of gender but to examine where the question has taken us thus far and then to move on to new areas of inquiry.

The Construction of Reality

Constructivism asserts that we do not discover reality, we invent it (Watzlawick, 1984). Our experience does not directly reflect what is out there but is a selecting, ordering, and organizing of it. Knowing is a search for "fitting" ways of behaving and thinking (Von Glaserfeld, 1984). Rather than passively observing reality, we actively construct the meanings that frame and organize our perceptions and experience. Thus, our understanding of reality is a representation, not an exact replica, of what is out there. Representations of reality are shared meanings that derive from shared language, history, and culture. Rorty (1979) suggests that the notion of accurate representation is a compliment we pay to those beliefs that are successful in helping us do what we want to do. The "realities" of social life are products of language and agreed-on meanings.

Constructivism challenges the scientific tradition of positivism, which holds that reality is fixed and can be observed directly, uninfluenced by the observer (Gergen, 1985; Sampson, 1985; Segal, 1986). As Heisenberg (1952) has pointed out, a truly objective world, devoid of all subjectivity, would have no one to observe it. Constructivism also challenges the presumption of positivist science that it is possible to distinguish facts from values. For constructivists, values and attitudes determine what are taken to be facts (Howard, 1985). It is not that formal laws and theories in psychology are wrong or useless; rather, as Kuhn (1962) asserted, they are explanations based on a set of agreed-on social conventions. Whereas positivism asks what are the facts, constructivism asks what are the assumptions; whereas positivism asks what are the answers, constructivism asks what are the questions.

The positivist tradition holds that science is the exemplar of the right use of reason, neutral in its methods, socially beneficial in its results (Flax, 1987). Historically, the scientific movement challenged the canons of traditional belief and the authority of church and state. Science was a reform movement that struggled to supplant faith as the sole source of knowledge by insisting on the unity of experience and knowing. For Western society today, science has largely displaced church and state authority so that *scientific* has itself become a euphemism for *proper*.

Constructivism holds that scientific knowledge, like all other knowledge, cannot be disinterested or politically neutral. In psychology, constructivism, drawing on the ideas of Bateson and Maturana, has influenced epistemological developments in systems theories of the family (Dell, 1985). Constructivist views have also been put forth in developmental psychology (Bronfenbrenner, Kessel, Kessen & White, 1986; Scarr, 1985), in the psychology of women (Unger, 1983, and this book), and in the study of human sexuality (Tiefer, 1987). Constructivist views also form the basis of the social constructionism movement in social psychology, which draws inspiration from symbolic anthropology, ethnomethodology, and related movements in sociology and anthropology (Gergen, 1985; Kessler & McKenna, 1978).

From a constructivist perspective, theories of gender, like all scientific theories, are representations of reality that are organized within particular assumptive frameworks and that reflect certain interests. Below, we examine gender theorizing in psychology and indicate some of the assumptions and issues that a constructivist approach makes apparent.

The Construction of Gender as Difference

From a constructivist standpoint, the real nature of male and female cannot be determined. Constructivism focuses our attention on representations of gender rather than on gender itself. We note first that most languages, including our own, are elaborately gendered. Gender differentiation is a preeminent phenomenon of symbolic life and communication in our society, although this is not the case in all languages and cultures. Nonetheless, the English language still lacks adequate terms for speaking of each gender. *Male-female* has the advantage of referring to individuals across the entire life span, but the terms imply biological characteristics and fail to distinguish humans from other species. *Men-women* is more restrictive, referring specifically to humans, but it has the disadvantage of omitting childhood and adolescence. In this chapter, we use *men* and *women* for the most part, but we use *male* and *female* when we wish to include individuals at any point in the life span.

The very term *gender* illustrates the power of linguistic categories to determine what we know of the world. The use of *gender* in contexts other than discussions of grammar is quite recent. *Gender* was appropriated by contemporary American feminists to refer to the social quality of distinctions between the sexes (Scott, 1985). *Gender* is used in contrast to terms like *sex* and *sexual difference* for the explicit purpose of creating a space in which socially mediated differences between men and women can be explored apart from biological differences (Unger, 1979). The germinal insight of feminist thought was the discovery that *woman* is a social category. So although sexual differences can be reduced to the reproductive system in males (sperm production) and females (ovulation, pregnancy, childbirth, and lactation), sex differences do not account for gender, for women's social, political, and economic subordination or women's child care responsibilities.

From the vantage point of constructivism, theories of gender are representations based on conventional distinctions. In our view, such theories embody one of two contrasting biases, alpha bias and beta bias (Hare-Mustin, 1987). Alpha bias is the tendency to exaggerate differences; beta bias is the tendency to minimize or ignore differences.

The alpha-beta schema is in some ways analogous to that in scientific hypothesis testing in experimental psychology and thus is a schema familiar to psychologists. In hypothesis testing, alpha or Type 1 error involves reporting a significant difference when one does not exist; beta or Type 2 error involves overlooking a significant difference when one does exist. In our formulation, the term *bias* refers not to the probability of error (which would imply that there is a correct position), but to a systematic slant or inclination to emphasize certain aspects of experience and overlook other aspects. This inclination or tendency is presumably related to the standpoint of the knower, that is, the position where he or she is located within and as part of the context. Thus, the standpoint of the knower necessarily shapes her or his view of reality. Far from deterring the knower from gaining knowledge, taking a standpoint can be a positive strategy for generating new knowledge (Hartsock, 1985). Our use of the term *bias* underscores our contention that all ideas about difference are social constructs; none can be mirrors of reality. Alpha and beta bias can be seen in representations of gender, race, class, age, and the like that either emphasize or overlook difference. Here we use the alpha-beta schema to examine recent efforts to theorize gender.

ALPHA BIAS

Alpha bias is the exaggeration of differences. The view of male and female as different and opposite and thus as having mutually exclusive qualities transcends Western culture and has deep historical roots. Ideas of male-female opposition are present in Eastern thought and throughout Western philosophy, including the writings of Aristotle, Aquinas, Bacon, and Descartes, as well as the writings of liberal theorists such as Locke and romanticists such as Rousseau (Grimshaw, 1986). Throughout Western history, woman has been regarded as the repository of nonmasculine traits, an "otherness" men assign to women.

The scientific model developed by Francis Bacon was based on the distinction between "male" reason and its "female" opposites—passion, lust, and emotion (Keller, 1985). Because women were restricted to the private sphere, they did not have access to the knowledge available in the public realm. The knowledge women did have, such as witchcraft, was disparaged or repudiated. As Evelyn Fox Keller points out, women's knowledge was associated with insatiable lust; men's knowledge was assumed to be chaste. In Bacon's model of science, nature was cast in the image of the female, to be subdued, subjected to the penetrating male gaze, and forced to yield up her secrets (cf. Keller, 1985; Merchant, 1980). Bacon's views are but one manifestation of the long-standing association of women with nature and emotion and men with reason, technology, and civilization (Ortner, 1974). The material body has been a symbol of human limitation and decay since at least early Christian times. Hence, men sought to be other than their bodies, to transcend their bodies. They dissociated themselves from their bodies and associated women with materiality, the sphere of nature, and the body (Butler, 1987). The opposition of reason and emotion, as well as the opposition of civilization and nature, emphasized in the Enlightenment, served in later times to reinforce liberalism's emphasis on rationality as the capacity that distinguishes humans from animals (Grimshaw, 1986).

In psychology, alpha bias can be readily seen in most psychodynamic theories. Freudian theory is not neutral about sexual differences but imposes meanings. It takes masculinity and male anatomy as the human standard; femininity and female anatomy are deviations from that standard. Thus, Freud characterized women's bodies as *not having* a penis rather than as *having* the female external genitalia. Similarly, he portrayed feminine character in terms of its deficiencies relative to masculine character. The Jungian idea of the animus and the anima also places the masculine and the feminine in opposition.

More recent psychodynamic theories also depict women as sharply divergent from men. For example, Erikson (1964) wrote that female identity is predicated on "inner space," a somatic design that "harbors . . . a biological, psychological, and ethical commitment to take care of human infancy. . ." (586), and a sensitive indwelling. Male identity is associated with "outer space," which involves intrusiveness, excitement, and mobility, leading to achievement, political domination, and adventure seeking. In Lacan's (1985) poststructuralist view, women are "outside" language, public discourse, culture, and the law. For Lacan, the female is defined not by what is, but by the absence or lack of the phallus as the prime signifier. In these ways psychodynamic theories overlook similarities between males and females and instead emphasize differences.

Parsons's sex-role theory, which dominated the social theories of the 1950s and 1960s, also emphasizes male-female differences (Parsons & Bales, 1955). The very language of sex-role theory powerfully conveys the sense that men's and women's roles are fixed and dichotomous, as well as separate and reciprocal (Thorne, 1982). Parsons asserted that men were instrumental and women were expressive, that is, men were task-oriented and women were oriented toward feelings and relationships. Parsons's sex-role theory was hailed as providing a scientific basis for relegating men and women to separate spheres. Men's nature suited them for paid work and public life; women's nature suited them for family work and home life. Thus women became first in "goodness" by putting their own needs secondary to those of their families and altruistically donating their services to others

(Lipman-Blumen, 1984). Parsons believed that separate spheres for men and women were functional in reducing competition and conflict in the family and thus preserving harmony. The role definitions that Parsons put forward came to serve as criteria for distinguishing normal individuals and families from those who were pathological or even pathogenic (cf. Broverman, Broverman, Clarkson, Rosenkrantz & Vogel, 1970). The criteria associated with sex-role differentiation continue to be applied to family structure and functioning in such theories as contemporary exchange theory (Nye, 1982) and structural family therapy (Minuchin, 1974).

Alpha bias, or the inclination to emphasize differences, can also be seen in feminist psychodynamic theories (cf. Chodorow, 1978; Eichenbaum & Orbach, 1983; Gilligan, 1982; Miller, 1986). According to Nancy Chodorow (1978), boys and girls undergo contrasting experiences of identity formation during their early years under the social arrangement in which the care of infants is provided exclusively by women. Her influential work, which is based on object-relations theory, argues that girls' early experiences involve similarity and attachment to their mothers while boys' early experiences emphasize difference, separateness, and independence. These experiences are thought to result in broad-ranging gender differences in identity, personality structure, and psychic needs in adulthood. Women develop a deep-seated motivation to have children, whereas men develop the capacity to participate in the alienating work structures of advanced capitalism. Thus, according to Chodorow, the social structure produces gendered personalities that reproduce the social structure. Although Chodorow locates the psychodynamics of personality development temporally and situationally in Western industrial capitalism, psychologists who draw on her work often overlook this point concerning the social context. Her work is used to assert that there are essential differences between women and men and to view these, rather than the social structure, as the basis for gender roles (cf. Chernin, 1986;

Eichenbaum & Orbach, 1983; Schlachet, 1984; Jordan & Surrey, 1986). In any case, both Chodorow's theory and the work of her followers emphasize gender difference and thus exemplify alpha bias.

In her approach to women's development, Carol Gilligan (1982) harks back to Parsons's duality, viewing women as relational and men as instrumental and rational. Her theory of women's moral development echoes some of the gender differences asserted by Freud (1964) and Erikson (1964). She describes female identity as rooted in connections to others and relationships. She views female morality as based on an ethic of care and responsibility rather than fairness and rights. Unlike Freud, however, she views women's differences from men in a positive light.

Both traditional psychodynamic theories and the recently developed feminist psychodynamic theories emphasize differences between men and women while overlooking the similarities between them. Whereas the emphasis on difference in traditional theories went hand in hand with a devaluation of what was seen as female, feminists' emphasis on difference is coupled with a positive evaluation of women's attributes. Their emphasis on women's unique capacities for relationships and on the richness of women's inner experience has been an important resource for the movement within feminism known as cultural feminism. Cultural feminism encourages the development and expression of a women's culture, celebrates the special qualities of women, and values relationships among women.

BETA BIAS

The inclination to ignore or minimize differences, *beta bias*, has been less prominent in psychological theory than alpha bias, and thus our treatment of it is necessarily briefer. One example of beta bias in theory development is the practice, common until recent decades, of drawing generalizations about human behavior, adult development, and personality from observations limited to males (Wallston, 1981). Male experience was assumed to represent all experience. This is an instance of beta bias insofar as generalizations about human experience based only on the male life course assume that women's experiences are no different than men's. Such generalizations offer only a partial view of humanity.

Another common instance of beta bias is the tendency to overlook both the differences in the social and economic resources that men and women typically have at their disposal as well as the differences in the social meanings and consequences of their actions. Thus, beta bias can be seen in social policies that provide equivalent benefits for men and women but overlook their disparate needs (Weitzman, 1985). Two examples, which we take up later, are comparable parental leave and no-fault divorce. Beta bias can also be seen in educational and therapeutic programs that focus on transforming the individual while leaving the social context unchanged. For example, some programs purport to groom women for personal or professional success by providing training in what are deemed male behaviors or skills, such as assertiveness, authoritative speech patterns, or certain managerial styles. Thus, if a woman wants to succeed as a manager, she is instructed to copy the demeanor and actions of successful men. Such programs presume that a certain manner of speaking or acting will elicit the same reaction from others regardless of the sex of the actor. This can be questioned (Gervasio & Crawford, 1989; Marecek & Hare-Mustin, 1987); for example, asking for a date, a classic task in assertiveness training, is judged differently for a woman than a man (Muehlenhard, 1983).

Beta bias can also be seen in theories of gender that represent masculine and feminine roles or traits as counterparts, as the construct of psychological androgyny does. The idea of masculinity and femininity as counterparts implies their symmetry and equivalence and thus obscures gender differences in power and social value. Sandra Bem's (1976) theory of psychological androgyny, which called for the creation of more balanced and healthy individuals by integrating positive masculine and feminine qualities, implied the equivalence of such qualities (Morawski, 1985; Worell, 1978).

Bem's original hypotheses suggested that individuals who identified themselves as highly feminine and those who identified themselves as highly masculine would be equally handicapped in performing "cross-sex" tasks and equally disadvantaged in terms of psychological well-being. But attempts to demonstrate this empirically did not yield such symmetrical effects (Morawski, 1987); rather, a masculine sex-role orientation tended to be associated with greater adaptiveness, as well as higher scores on indices of self-esteem and other aspects of psychological well-being. This is perhaps not surprising: If society values masculine qualities more highly than feminine qualities, individuals who have (or perceive themselves to have) those qualities should feel better about themselves. This is not to say that every quality associated with masculinity is regarded as positive. Aggression, for instance, is deplored outside of combat situations and competitive sports.

Beta bias can also be seen in theories of family functioning that ignore gender. In all societies, four primary axes along which hierarchies are established are class, race, gender, and age. Within families, class and race usually are constant, but gender and age vary. Family systems theories, however, disregard gender and view generation (that is, age) as the central organizing principle in the family (Hare-Mustin, 1987). Such theories emphasize the importance of the boundaries that define the differences in power and responsibility between the parental generation and the children. In so doing, they deflect attention from questions about the distribution of power and resources *within* generations of a family. Are mothers as powerful as fathers? Are daughters afforded the same resources and degree of autonomy as sons? By regarding all members of a generation as equal interacting participants in the family system, systems theories put forward a neutered representation of family life (Libow, 1985).

The Question of Utility

Rather than debate the correctness of various representations of gender, the "true" nature of which cannot be known, constructivism turns to the utility or consequences of these representations. How, we ask, do representations of gender provide the meanings and symbols that organize scientific and therapeutic practice in psychology? What are the consequences of representing gender in ways that either emphasize or minimize male-female differences? We use the alpha-beta schema as a framework for discussing the utility of gender theories.

THE UTILITY OF ALPHA BIAS

Because alpha bias has been the prevailing representation of gender we take up the question of its utility first. Alpha bias has had a number of effects on our understanding of gender. An important positive consequence of alpha bias, or focusing on differences between women and men, is that it has allowed some theorists to assert the worth of certain so-called feminine qualities. This assertion has the positive effect of countering the cultural devaluation of women and encouraging greater self-acceptance among women (Echols, 1983). Further, the focus on women's special qualities by some feminists has also prompted a critique of those cultural values that excuse or even encourage aggression, extol the pursuit of self-interest, and foster narrow individualism. It has furnished an impetus for the development of a feminist social ethics and for a variety of related philosophical endeavors (Eisenstein, 1983). The emphasis on women's differences from men fosters a corresponding appreciation of the commonalities women share, an appreciation that can help to generate positive emotional bonds among women. Sisterhood and solidarity have spurred collective action by women to gain recognition and power.

Unfortunately, exaggerating gender difference does not always support the aims of feminism. By construing women as different and devaluing them, alpha bias fosters solidarity between men by construing women as a deviant out-group, which can then be devalued. In Durkheim's terms, deviance supports in-group solidarity. Defining a sharp boundary between male and female supports the status quo by exacerbating male fears of being viewed as feminine. This serves to enforce conformity by males to masculine stereotypes. Moreover, exaggerating women's difference from men fosters the view of woman as the Other (Beauvoir, 1953). Further, this distancing and alienating view of women by the dominant male culture opens the way to treating women as objects, as is apparent in certain pornographic images and in much of the physical and sexual abuse of females.

Alpha bias also supports the status quo by denying that change is needed in the structure of work and family life (Gilder, 1987; Marshner, 1982). So, for example, traditionalists assert that women are not as intellectually capable as men, women are temperamentally better suited for care-taking roles and, as was argued in the Sears sex discrimination case, women prefer not to undertake stereotyped male roles (Erikson, 1964; Rosenberg, 1986; Rossi, 1984). Women's presumed differences from men are used to justify unequal treatment. Yet, as Patricia Mills (1987) suggests, it is women's confinement to the family that secures her difference. The possibility that it is the unequal treatment that might lead to the apparent differences between men and women is hidden from view.

The idea that male and female are opposites masks inequality between men and women as well as conflict between them. By construing rationality as an essential male quality and relatedness as an essential female quality, for example, such theories as those of Gilligan and Parsons conceal the possibility that those qualities result from social inequities and power differences. Men's propensity to reason from principles might stem from the fact that the principles were formulated to promote their interests; women's concern with relationships can be understood as a need to please others that arises from lack of power (Hare-Mustin & Marecek, 1986). Typically, those in power advocate rules, discipline, control, and rationality, while those without power espouse relatedness and compassion. Thus, in husband-wife conflicts, husbands call on rules and logic, whereas wives call on caring. But, when women are in the dominant position, as in parent-child conflicts, they emphasize rules while their children appeal for sympathy and understanding or for exceptions based on special circumstances. This suggests that rationality and relatedness are not gender-linked traits, but rather stances evoked by one's position in a social hierarchy.

Others have offered related accounts of how women's greater concern with relationships might be a consequence of women's position in the social hierarchy rather than an essential female attribute. Wilden (1972), for example, proposes that low social status imparts a need to monitor where one stands in a relationship: "Anyone in a social relationship which defines him or her as inferior must necessarily be much more concerned to discover what the relationship is about than to communicate or receive any particular message within it" (297).

Women's caring is but one example of a behavior that has been represented as a gender difference but can be more adequately represented as a way of negotiating from a position of low power. As Bernice Lott discusses below, many other differences between men and women are best construed as stances associated with their relative positions in the social hierarchy rather than as differences of gender per se. These alternative accounts open the way for psychologists to consider why every woman is not concerned with caring and relationships and why some men are.

Feminist psychodynamic theories make assertions of extensive male-female personality differences throughout life. Even when these theories applaud the personality attributes of women, they can serve as justification for restricting individuals to a particular social place. Further, critics have challenged the idea that a brief period in infancy could be responsible for creating the broad-ranging differences that psychodynamic theorists assert and overriding subsequent experiences in human development. Critics similarly challenge whether personality differences alone could be responsible for the gendering of all social institutions throughout history (cf. Kagan, 1984; Lott, 1987; Scott, 1985); that is, feminist psychodynamic theories have been criticized for overplaying the influence of early experience and individual personality to the neglect of economic conditions, social role conditioning, and historical change.

A further question has been raised as to whether changes in patterns of infant care-giving such as Nancy Chodorow (1978) and Dorothy Dinnerstein (1976) propose are sufficient to undermine gender difference and thereby to effect social transformation. There is an uncomfortable literalism in imputing such power to such a small segment of experience. Joan Scott (1985) has drawn attention to this problem in terms of representing the well-ordered family as the foundation of a well-ordered society.

In focusing on the question of why *differences* exist, feminist psychodynamic theories disregard the question of why *domination* exists. Iris Young (1983) points out that psychodynamic theories posit a masculine desire for power but fail to account for how men achieve power. The identification of a problem does not constitute an explanation.

Alpha bias, the exaggerating of differences between groups, has the additional consequence of ignoring or minimizing the extent of differences (or variability) among members of each group. The focus on Woman obliterates the sight of women. Further, such outgroups as women are viewed as more homogeneous than dominant groups (Park & Rothbart, 1982). Differences among men are readily identified, but all women are regarded as pretty much the same. Thus, men are viewed as individuals, but women are viewed as women. As a result, most psychological theories of gender have been slow to concern themselves with differences among women that are due to race, ethnicity, class, age, marital status, and a variety of social circumstances.

Another consequence of alpha bias is the tendency to view men and women not only as different but as opposite. The conception of masculine and feminine as embodying opposite and mutually exclusive traits is not only prevalent in the culture at large, but it has been embedded in certain well-established psychological tests. These include the Terman-Miles (1936) Masculinity-Femininity Personality Scale (M-F), the California Personality Inventory (Gough, 1964), and the Minnesota Multiphasic Personality Inventory (Hathaway & McKinley, 1943). The existence of these scales testifies to fifty years of psychological effort to evaluate the constructs of masculinity and femininity, an unrelenting search for the presumed core of what defines masculine and feminine (Morawski, 1987). Anne Constantinople (1973) has questioned the usefulness of the M-F construct, pointing out the vague definitions used in test construction: M-F is defined as whatever masculinity-femininity tests measure. She concluded that such tests merely measured the differences in the responses of men and women.

These tests are constructed so that a respondent must disavow feminine qualities in order to be categorized as masculine and vice versa. Thus, masculinity-femininity is represented as a single bipolar dimension, a unitary continuum. Masculinity and femininity are defined in terms of one another; what one is, the other is not.

Such dichotomies caricature human experience; for example, to maintain the illusion of male autonomy, the contribution of women's work at home and in the workplace must be overlooked. Feminist social scientists have observed that women and the family have been asked to compensate for the indifference and hostility of the outer world. Thus, the home is viewed as a haven (Lasch, 1977), but it is actually that *women* are the haven for men. The home is a metaphor that serves to obscure men's dependence on women and thus perpetuates the illusion of male autonomy. Similarly, the corporate world is seen as the locus of men's achievement and independence, but this overlooks the contribution of women. The extent to which female support personnel, such as secretaries and receptionists, cover up their bosses' absences and shortcomings, administer their work day, and provide personal service is obscured. In both cases, women are expected to provide for men's physical needs and mediate their social relations.

The portrayal of women as relational also ignores the complexity of their experiences. Rearing children involves achievement, and nurturing others involves power over those in one's care (Hare-Mustin & Marecek, 1986). When gender is represented as dichotomized traits, the extent to which presumed opposites include aspects of each other is overlooked. It is of interest to note that when women enter the "man's world" of business, they often flounder at first because they assume it operates according to formal rules and principles; they underestimate the importance of informal relationships, reciprocal favors, and personal influence.

Gender dichotomies regarding work and housework also caricature the actual experiences of both housewives and working women. In industrialized societies one's value is associated with the money one earns. Those who do not earn money—housewives, children, and old people—have an ambiguous status (Hare-Mustin, 1978). The contemporary focus on industrial production has led to the belief that households no longer produce anything important, and consequently that housewives no longer have much to do. But what exists is better represented as a two-tiered production system in which work for money is carried on outside the home while a familial production system continues within. As Ruth Schwartz Cowan (1983) has pointed out, women produce without payment meals, clean laundry, healthy children, well-fed adults, and transportation for goods and people at a level unknown in past times. Yet paid workers are seen as productive and housewives are not.

The view of male and female as opposite also supports the idea of separate spheres. The idea of separate spheres lives on, even though the majority of women are now in the paid labor force and operate in both spheres. A false symmetry embodied in the notion of separate spheres obscures women's dual roles and work overload (Hare-Mustin, 1988).

The representation of gender as dichotomies or opposites has had a long history in human thought. Even the autonomy-relatedness dichotomy was foreshadowed by earlier dichotomies such as agentic-communal (Bakan, 1966) and instrumental-expressive (Parsons & Bales, 1955). Indeed, man-woman may serve as a universal binary opposition. If so, this is not the result simply of a faulty definition, but as Wilden (1972) says, of prevailing ideology. The representation of gender as opposition has its source not in some accidental confusion of logical typing, but in the dominant group's interest in preserving the status quo. Calling the psychosocial and economic relations of men and women *opposition* imputes symmetry to a relationship that is unequal. As Dorothy Dinnerstein (1976) pointed out, women have been discontent with the double standard, but men on the whole are satisfied with it. Further, denying the interrelationships between male and female serves to maintain inequality.

Alpha bias, or exaggerating differences, thus plays an important role in preserving the status quo. Perhaps for this reason, the mass media often promulgate representations of gender that emphasize difference and underplay those that minimize difference. As Martha Mednick (1989) documents, the media have given extensive coverage to women's difference, such as their "fear of success," their lack of a "math gene," and their "different voice." Similarly, popular self-help books appeal to women's supposedly greater expressiveness, empathy, and sensitivity, while holding women responsible for all that goes wrong in intimate relationships (Worell, 1988). Points of similarity between women and men do not make news, nor are refutations of exaggerated claims of male-female difference considered newsworthy.

THE UTILITY OF BETA BIAS

Beta bias, or minimizing differences, also has consequences for understanding gender, but its consequences have received less attention. On the positive side, equal treatment under the law has enabled women to gain greater access to educational and occupational opportunities, as well as equal pay for equal work. This is largely responsible for the improvement in the status of some women over the last two decades (Dionne, 1989).

Arguing for no differences between women and men, however, draws attention away from women's special needs and from differences in power and resources between women and men. A ready example is seen in the statutes legislating equal pay for equal work, which have had relatively little effect on equalizing incomes across gender. This is because most women work in female-identified sectors of the economy in which wages are low. In a society in which one group holds most of the power, ostensibly neutral actions usually benefit members of that group. In Lenore Weitzman's (1985) research, for example, no-fault divorce settlements were found to have raised men's standard of living 42 percent while lowering that of women and children 73 percent. Another example is the effort to promote public policies granting comparable parental leave for mothers and fathers of newborns. Such policies overlook the physical effects of giving birth from which women need to recuperate and the demands of breastfeeding that are met uniquely by women who nurse their infants.

Giving birth is, paradoxically, both an ordinary event and an extraordinary one, as well as the only visible biological link in the kinship system. The failure of the workplace to accommodate women's special needs associated with childbirth represents beta bias, in which male needs and behaviors set the norm, and women's unique experiences are overlooked.

In therapy, treating men and women as if they were equal is not always equitable (Gilbert, 1980; Margolin, Talovic, Fernandez & Onorato, 1983). In marital and family therapy, treating partners as equals can overlook structural inequalities within the relationship. Some family systems theorists have tried to dismiss the concept of power as an epistemological error, arguing that both partners in a relationship contribute to the maintenance of the relationship. The notion of reciprocity, however, implies that the participants are not only mutually involved but equally involved in maintaining the interaction, and that they can equally influence its outcome (MacKinnon & Miller, 1987). As Virginia Goldner points out, this is not unlike the "kind of moral relativism in which the elegant truth that master and slave are psychologically interdependent drifts into the morally repugnant and absurd notion that the two are therefore equals" (1987, 111). As long as the social status and economic resources of the husband exceed those of the wife, marital contracts and quid pro quo bargaining strategies for resolving conflicts between partners will not lead to equitable results. *Sex-fair* or *gender-neutral* therapies that advocate nonpreferential and nondifferential treatment of women and men to achieve formal equality can inadvertently foster inequality (Bernal & Ysern, 1986; Jacobson, 1983; Marecek & Kravetz, 1977).

Our purpose in examining representations of gender has not been to catalogue every possible consequence of alpha and beta bias but to demonstrate that representation is never neutral. From the vantage point of constructivism, theories of gender can be seen as representations that construct our knowledge of men and women and inform social and scientific practice. Gender selects and gives meaning to sexual differences. Deconstruction provides another approach for examining representation and meaning in language. We now turn to the ways in which deconstruction can be used to examine the meanings of gender in the practice of therapy.

Deconstruction

Just as constructivism denies that there is a single fixed reality, the approach to literary interpretation known as deconstruction denies that texts have a single fixed meaning. Deconstruction offers a means of examining the way language operates outside our everyday awareness to create meaning (Culler, 1982). Deconstruction is generally applied to literary texts, but it can be applied equally to scientific texts, or, as we suggest below, to therapeutic discourse.

A primary tenet of deconstruction is that texts can generate a variety of meanings in excess of what is intended. In this view, language is not a stable system of correspondences of words to objects but "a sprawling limitless web where there is constant circulation of elements" (Eagleton, 1983, 129). The meaning of a word depends on its relation to other words, specifically, its difference from other words.

Deconstruction is based on the philosophy of Derrida, who moves beyond the structuralist thesis that posits closed language systems. Derrida has pointed out that Western thought is built on a series of interrelated hierarchical oppositions, such as reason-emotion, presence-absence, fact-value, good-evil, male-female (Culler, 1982). In each pair, the terms take their meaning from their opposition to (or difference from) each other; each is defined in terms of what the other is not. The first member of each pair is considered "more valuable and a better guide to the truth" (Nehamas, 1987, 32). But Derrida challenges both the opposition and the hierarchy, drawing attention to how each term contains elements of the other and depends for its meaning on the other. It is only by marginalizing their similarities that their meaning as opposites is stabilized and the value of one over the other is sustained.

Just as the meaning of a word partly depends on what the word is not, the meaning of a text partly depends on what the text does not say. Deconstructive readings thus rely on gaps, inconsistencies, and contradictions in the text, and even on metaphorical associations. Deconstruction can serve as a tool for probing what psychology has represented as oppositions, such as autonomy-nurturance, instrumentality-expressiveness, mental health-mental illness. Our intention here is not to provide a detailed explication of deconstruction but to suggest some ways that it can be used to understand meaning and gender. Our focus here is on psychotherapy.

Therapy, Meaning, and Change

Therapy centers on meaning, and language is its medium. Therapy is an oral mode, and narratives, proverbs, metaphors, and interpretations are its substance. The metaphorical language used in therapy to represent the world is a way to try to comprehend partially what cannot be comprehended totally (Spence, 1987). A deconstructivist view of the process of therapy draws attention to the play of meanings in the therapist-client dialogue and the way a therapist poses alternative meanings to create possibilities for change. This renegotiation of the client's meanings can take place explicitly, as in psychodynamic therapies, cognitive therapy, or rational-emotive therapy. Or it can take place implicitly, as when a behavior therapist instructs a client on how to bring anxiety symptoms under voluntary control, or a pharmacotherapist reattributes symptoms of depression to disturbances in body chemistry. The therapeutic process can be seen as one in which the client asks the therapist to reveal something about the client beyond the client's awareness, something that the client does not know.

Clients in therapy talk not about actual experiences but about reconstructed memories that resemble the original experiences only in certain ways. The client's story conforms to prevailing narrative conventions (Spence, 1982). This means that the client's representation of events moves further and further away from the experience and into a descriptive mode. The client as narrator is a creator of his or her world, not a disinterested observer.

The therapist's task of listening and responding to the client's narratives is akin to a deconstructive reading of a text. Both seek subtexts and multiple levels of meaning. Just as deconstructive readings disrupt the frame of reference that organizes conventional meanings of a text, so a therapist's interventions disrupt the frame of reference within which the client customarily sees the world. Such disruptions enable new meanings to emerge (Watzlawick, Weakland & Fisch, 1974). As a multiplicity of meanings becomes apparent through such therapist actions as questioning, explaining, interpreting, and disregarding, more possibilities for change emerge. The deconstructive process is most apparent in psychoanalysis, but, indeed, all therapy involves changing meaning as part of changing behavior. The metaphor of therapy as healing is an idealization that obscures another metaphor, that therapists manipulate meanings. These metaphors are not contrary to each other; rather, as part of helping clients change, therapists change clients' meanings (Frank, 1976; Haley, 1987).

GENDER AND MEANING IN THERAPY

Just as a poem can have many readings, a client's experience can have many meanings. Certain meanings are privileged, however, because they conform to the explanatory systems of the dominant culture. As a cultural institution whose purpose is to help individuals adapt to their social condition, therapy usually reflects and promulgates such privileged meanings. But some therapists, such as radical therapists and feminist therapists, bring a social critique to their work. Such therapists, rather than attempting to bring clients' meanings in line with those of the culture, disrupt the meanings privileged by the culture. Below, we examine certain privileged and marginalized meanings in relation to gender issues, issues that have been at the center of considerable debate among therapists and in society at large (Brodsky & Hare-Mustin, 1980).

We begin with Freud's classic case of Dora (1963). When we look at Dora's case from a deconstructive perspective, we can see it as a therapist's attempt to adjust the meaning a client attached to her experience to match the prevailing meanings of the patriarchal society in which she lived. A "landmark of persuasion unsurpassed in clinical literature" is the way Spence described Dora's case (1987, 122). Dora viewed the sexual attentions of her father's associate, Herr K, as unwanted and uninvited. She responded to them with revulsion. Freud insistently reframed the sexual encounters with Herr K as desired and desirable for a fourteen-year-old girl and interpreted Dora's revulsion as a disguise for her true state of sexual arousal. When Dora refused to accept Freud's construction, he labeled her as vengeful and declared therapy a failure.

From our vantage point ninety years after Dora's encounter with Freud, the case shows how meanings embedded in the dominant culture often go unrecognized or unacknowledged. Freud evidently viewed Herr K's lecherous advances as acceptable behavior, although Herr K was married and Dora was only fourteen and the daughter of a close family friend. We can surmise that the cultural belief in the primacy of men's sexual needs prevented Freud from seeing Dora's revulsion as genuine.

Freud's analysis of Dora provides an example of how a therapist attempts to reaffirm privileged meanings and marginalize and discourage other meanings, to fill in the gaps and make intelligible a narrative. Where does Dora leave off and Freud begin? The many meanings of Dora's behavior—and Freud's as well—are evident in the numerous reanalyses, filmic representations, and critical literary readings of the case, which continue to be produced up to the present day.

Conventional meanings of gender are embedded in the language of therapy. Like all language, the language used in therapy can be thought of as metaphoric: it selects, emphasizes, suppresses, and organizes certain features of experience, and thus it imparts meaning to experience; for example, *Oedipus complex* imposes the complexity of adult erotic feelings onto the experiences of small children and emphasizes the male and the primacy of the phallus. The metaphor of the family ledger in family therapy implies that family relations are (or should be) organized as mercantile exchanges and centered on male achievements (Boszormenyi-Nagy & Sparks, 1973).

Dominant meanings are often embedded in everyday language and commonplace metaphors. By challenging linguistic conventions and unpacking metaphors, therapists can disrupt these meanings. With respect to gender, for example, a therapist can unpack the metaphor of family harmony and expose the gender hierarchy by pointing out that accord within the family often is maintained by women's acquiescence and accommodation (Haavind, 1984; Hare-Mustin, 1978; 1987). Moreover, the stress generated by women's prescribed family roles is often marginalized or overlooked (Baruch, Biener & Barnett, 1987). Psychologists studying stress have focused largely on men with men's workplace identified as a stressor. The home, in contrast, has been viewed as a benign environment in which one recuperates from work. This picture is drawn from a male perspective. For most women, the home *is* the workplace or at least one of their workplaces. Further, women's roles associated with the home are not free of undue stress. Family harmony involves a woman's pleasing a husband and keeping a home attractive, activities that are frequently incompatible with meeting children's needs (Piotrkowski & Repetti, 1984).

In unpacking the metaphor of family loyalty, the therapist can draw attention to the way the needs of some family members are subordinated to those of dominant members in the name of loyalty. In maintaining the ties in the family network, women provide for others while their own needs go unmet (Belle, 1982).

The metaphor of women's dependency can also serve to conceal the extent to which women as wives and mothers provide for the needs of men and boys. Women have traditionally been characterized as dependent, but Harriet Lerner (1983) raises the provocative questions: Have women been dependent enough? Have they been able to call on others to meet their needs? As Westkott (1986) observes, the assumption of male entitlement to unconditional nurturance from females is rarely questioned; nor is it labeled as dependency and regarded as a psychological problem.

Finally, both private concerns with preserving the family and public rhetoric about the decline of the family can be challenged by drawing attention to the use of "the family" as a metaphor for male dominance (Pogrebin, 1983). Is it the family that is threatened or just a form of the family that supports men's greater power and status? Judith Stacey (1983) also draws attention to the way feminist theory has deconstructed the family as a natural unit and reconstructed it as a social unit.

As we have shown, the resemblance of therapeutic discourse to narrative offers the possibility of using deconstruction as a resource for understanding meaning and the process of therapy. Therapy typically confirms privileged meanings, but deconstruction directs attention to marginalized meanings. Doing therapy from a feminist standpoint is like the deconstructionist's "reading as a woman" (Culler, 1982). The therapist exposes gender-related meanings that reside in such culturally embedded metaphors as family harmony but go unacknowledged in the conventional understanding of those metaphors. These new meanings can change the ways that clients understand their own behaviors and the behaviors of others—the *click* experience that women in the consciousness-raising groups of the 1960s and 1970s so often reported. New meanings allow and often impel clients to make changes in their lives.

Paradoxes in Gender Theorizing

The issue of gender differences has been a divisive one for feminist scholars. Some believe that affirming difference affirms women's value and special nature. Others believe that insisting on equality (that is, no difference) is necessary for social change and the redistribution of power and privilege. But both ways of representing gender involve paradoxes. Like every representation, both conceal as they reveal. A paradox is contrary (*para*) to received opinion (*doxa*), a logical impossibility or a result contrary to what is desired.

One such paradox is that efforts to affirm the special value of women's experience and to valorize women's inner life turn attention away from efforts to change the material conditions of women's lives (Fine, 1985; Russ, 1986; Tobias, 1986). Feelings of emotional intensity may not lead to an understanding of oneself or of society. A change in consciousness and symbolic life alone does not necessarily produce a change in the social conditions of individuals' lives and institutional structures.

Another paradox arises from the assertion of a female way of knowing, involving intuition and experiential understanding rather than logical abstraction. This assertion implies that all other ways of knowing are male. If taken to an extreme, the privileging of emotion and bodily knowledge over reason can lead to the rejection of rational thought. It can also be taken to imply that women are incapable of rational thought and of acquiring the knowledge of the dominant culture.

There is yet another paradox. Qualities such as caring, expressiveness, and concern for relationships are extolled as women's superior virtues and the wellspring of public regeneration and morality. But they are also seen as arising from women's subordination (Miller, 1976) and from women's being outsiders and oppressed. Thus has Bertrand Russell spoken of the superior virtue of the oppressed. When we extol such qualities as women's caring, do we necessarily also extol women's subordination

(Echols, 1983)? Joan Ringleheim (1985) has suggested that the idealization of women's experience serves as a palliative for oppression. If subordination makes women better people, then the perpetuation of women's so-called goodness would seem to require continued subordination.

It is not only alpha bias that leads to paradoxes and logical confusion. Beta bias also can. Saying that women are as good as men is a statement of self-acceptance and pride for some women. But asserting that women are equal to men is not the same as asserting that women and men are equal; it reveals that *man* is the hidden referent in our language and culture. As Dale Spender (1984) points out, "women can only aspire to be as good as a man, there is no point in trying to be as good as a woman" (201). Paradoxically, this attempt at denying differences reaffirms male behavior as the standard against which all behavior is judged.

There is a paradox faced by any social change movement, including feminism: its critique is necessarily determined by the nature of the prevailing social system, and its meanings are embedded in that system. Sennett (1980) has observed a further paradox, that even when one's response to authority is defiance, that stance serves to confirm authority just as compliance does. Thus, the feminist critique simultaneously protests and protects the status quo. In this regard, Dorothy Dinnerstein (1976) has suggested that woman is not really the enemy of the system but its loyal opposition.

Moreover, feminist separatism, the attempt to avoid male influence by separating from men, leaves intact the larger system of male control in the society. Separatism can provide space for self-affection and woman-to-woman bonding, but as an ultimate goal it is caught as a mirror image of the masculine reality it is trying to escape (Cornell & Thurschwell, 1987).

The meaning of gender as male-female difference presents us with paradoxes. Whether such representations of gender emphasize difference or minimize it, they are fraught with logical contradictions and hidden meanings. The representation of gender as male-female difference obscures and marginalizes the interrelatedness and commonalities of women and men. It also obscures institutional sexism and the extent of male authority. Just as our examination of the utility of alpha bias and beta bias revealed no clear answer for those who ask the question of which is better, so too the paradoxes that arise reveal further complexities and contradictions. Can we look beyond these representations to new ways of understanding gender?

Conclusion

Male-female difference is a problematic and paradoxical way to construe gender. What we see is that alpha and beta bias have similar assumptive frameworks despite their diverse emphases. Both take the male as the standard of comparison. Both construct gender as attributes of individuals, not as the ongoing relations of men and women. Neither effectively challenges the gender hierarchy, and ultimately neither transcends the status quo. They are changes within the larger system of assumptions, but they leave the system itself unchanged. The multiple representations all frame the problem of what gender is in such a way that the solution is "more of the same" (Watzlawick, Weakland & Fisch, 1974).

Gender is not a property of individuals but a socially prescribed relationship, a process, and a social construction. Like race and class, however, gender cannot be renounced voluntarily. Representing gender as a continuum of psychological difference serves to simplify and purify the concept of gender. The riddle of gender is presumed to be solved when heterogeneous material is reduced to the homogeneity of logical thought (Gallop, 1982). To establish a dichotomy is to avoid complexity. The idea of gender as opposites obscures the complexity of human action and shields both men and women from the discomforting recognition of inequality.

The issue of difference is salient for men in a way that it is not for women. Those who are dominant have an interest in emphasizing those differences that reaffirm their superiority and in denying their similarity to subordinate groups. By representing nonsymmetrical relationships as symmetrical, those who are dominant obscure the unequal social arrangements that perpetuate male dominance. Thus, notions of gender that are part of our cultural heritage rely on defensive masculine models of gender (Chodorow, 1979). In accepting male-female difference as the meaning of gender, feminists have acceded to the construction of reality of the dominant group, "a gentle slide into the prevailing hegemony" (Bouchier, 1979, 397).

Even when differences are minimized and gender is represented as male-female similarity, equality remains elusive. Male themes and male views are presented as human experience. As Sandra Harding (1986) has observed, women are asked to degender themselves for a masculine version of experience without asking for a similar degendering of men. Even women's need to define themselves derives from and is perpetuated by their being the nondominant group. The dominant group does not define itself with respect to its group or order. Thus men do not refer to their masculine status, they do not add "as a man." But women speak "as a woman." Specifying "as a woman" reserves generality for men.

Deconstruction focuses attention on oppositions and hidden meanings in language. Language mirrors social relations, but it is also recursive on the social experiences that generate it. Thus, from a postmodernist perspective, there is no one right view of gender. Each view is partial and will present certain paradoxes. Feminist psychology has concentrated on male-female difference. Though the remapping of difference could go further, such a map of difference, even if perfected, will never reveal the entire terrain of gender. A map is not the terrain. Rather a map offers a construction of the terrain. With regard to gender, there are other maps to be drawn. For instance, some would map gender in terms of the principles that organize male-female relations in particular cultures (Stacey & Thorne, 1985). Some would map gender in terms of the discourses through which men and women position one another and define themselves (Hollway, 1984). Other maps, charting gender in yet other terms, are still to be invented.

Postmodernism accepts multiplicity, randomness, incoherence, indeterminacy, and paradox, which positivist paradigms are designed to exclude. Postmodernism creates distance from the seemingly fixed language of established meanings and fosters skepticism about the fixed nature of reality. Recognizing that meaning is what we agree on, postmodernism describes a system of possibilities. Constructing gender is a process, not an answer. In using a postmodernist approach, we open the possibility of theorizing gender in heretofore unimagined ways. Postmodernism allows us to see that as observers of gender we are also its creators.

REFERENCES

Andersen, M. L. (1983). *Thinking about women: Sociological and feminist perspectives.* New York: Macmillan.

Bakan, D. (1966). *The duality of human existence.* Chicago: Rand McNally.

Barthes, R. (1972). *Mythologies* (A. Lavers, Trans.). New York: Hill & Wang. (Original work published 1957.)

Baruch, G. K., Biener, L., & Barnett, R. C. (1987). Woman and gender in research on work and family stress. *American Psychologist, 42,* 130–36.

Beauvoir, S. de. (1953). *The second sex* (H. M. Parshley, Trans. & Ed.). New York: Knopf.

Belenky, M. F., Clinchy, B. M., Goldberger, N. R. & Tarule, J. M. (1986). *Women's ways of knowing: Development of self, voice, and mind.* New York: Basic Books.

Belle, D. (1982). Social ties and social support. In D. Belle (Ed.), *Lives in stress: Women and depression* (133–44). Beverly Hills: Sage.

Bem, S. L. (1976). Probing the promise of androgyny. In A. G. Kaplan & J. P.

Bean (Eds.), *Beyond sex-role stereotypes: Readings toward a psychology of androgyny* (48–62). Boston: Little, Brown.

Bernal, G. & Ysern, E. (1986). Family therapy and ideology. *Journal of Marital and Family Therapy, 12,* 129–35.

Bloom, A. H. (1981). *The linguistic shaping of thought.* Hillsdale, NJ: Erlbaum.

Boszormenyi-Nagy, I. & Sparks, G. M. (1973). *Invisible loyalties.* New York: Harper & Row.

Bouchier, D. (1979). The deradicalisation of feminism: Ideology and utopia. *Sociology, 13,* 387–402.

Brodsky, A. M., & Hare-Mustin, R. T. (1980). *Women and psychotherapy: An assessment of research and practice.* New York: Guilford.

Bronfenbrenner, U., Kessel, F., Kessen, W. & White, S. (1986). Toward a critical social history of developmental psychology: A propaedeutic discussion. *American Psychologist, 41,* 1218–30.

Broverman, I. K., Broverman, D. M., Clarkson, F. E., Rosenkrantz, P. & Vogel, S. R. (1970). Sex role stereotypes and clinical judgments of mental health. *Journal of Consulting Psychology, 34,* 1–7.

Bruner, J. (1986). *Actual minds, possible worlds.* Cambridge, MA: Harvard University Press.

Butler, J. (1987). Variations on sex and gender. In S. Benhabib & D. Cornell (Eds.), *Feminism as critique: On the politics of gender* (128–42). Minneapolis: University of Minnesota Press.

Chernin, K. (1986). *The hungry self: Women, eating, and identity.* New York: Perennial Library.

Chodorow, N. (1978). *The reproduction of mothering.* Berkeley: University of California Press.

Chodorow, N. (1979). Feminism and difference: Gender, relation, and difference in psychoanalytic perspective. *Socialist Review, 9* (4), 51–70.

Constantinople. A. (1973). Masculinity-femininity: An exception to a famous dictum? *Psychological Bulletin, 80,* 389–407.

Cornell, D. & Thurschwell, A. (1987). Feminism, negativity, intersubjectivity. In S. Benhabib & D. Cornell (Eds.), *Feminism as critique: On the politics of gender* (143–62). Minneapolis: University of Minnesota Press.

Cowan, R. S. (1983). *More work for mother: The ironies of household technology from open hearth to microwave.* New York: Basic Books.

Culler, J. (1982). *On deconstruction: Theory and criticism after structuralism.* Ithaca, NY: Cornell University Press.

Deaux, K. (1984). From individual differences to social categories: Analysis of a decade's research on gender. *American Psychologist, 39,* 105–16.

Dell, P. F. (1985). Understanding Bateson and Maturana: Toward a biological foundation for the social sciences. *Journal of Marital and Family Therapy, 11*, 1–20.

Dinnerstein, D. (1976). *The mermaid and the minotaur.* New York: Harper & Row.

Dionne, E. J. (1989, August 22). Struggle for work and family fueling women's movement. *New York Times*, A1, A18.

Eagleton, T. (1983). *Literary theory: An introduction.* Minneapolis: University of Minnesota Press.

Eagly, A. H. & Crowley, M. (1986). Gender and helping behavior: A meta-analytic review of the social psychological literature. *Psychological Bulletin, 100*, 283–308.

Eagly, A. H. & Steffen, V. J. (1986). Gender and aggressive behavior: A meta-analytic review of the social psychological literature. *Psychological Bulletin, 100*, 309–30.

Eccles, J. S. (1989). Bringing young women to math and science. In M. Crawford & M. Gentry (Eds.) *Gender and thought* (36–58). New York: Springer-Verlag.

Eccles, J. & Jacobs, J. (1986). Social forces shape math participation. *Signs, 11*, 368–80.

Echols, A. (1983). The new feminism of yin and yang. In A. Snitow, C. Stansell & S. Thompson (Eds.), *Powers of desire: The politics of sexuality* (440–59). New York: Monthly Review Press.

Eichenbaum, L. & Orbach, S. (1983). *Understanding women: A feminist psychoanalytic approach.* New York: Basic Books.

Eisenstein, H. (1983). *Contemporary feminist thought.* Boston: G. K. Hall.

Erikson, E. H. (1964). Inner and outer space: Reflections on womanhood. *Daedelus, 93*, 582–606.

Fine, M. (1985). Reflections on a feminist psychology of women. *Psychology of Women Quarterly, 9*, 167–83.

Flax, J. (1987). Postmodernism and gender relations in feminist theory. *Signs, 12*, 621–43.

Foucault, M. (1973). *The order of things.* New York: Vintage.

Frank, J. D. (1987). Psychotherapy, rhetoric, and hermeneutics: Implications for practice and research. *Psychotherapy, 24*, 293–302.

Freud, S. (1963). *Dora: An analysis of a case of hysteria.* New York: Collier Books. (Original work published 1905.)

Freud, S. (1964). Some psychical consequences of the anatomical distinction between the sexes. In J. Strachey (Ed. and Trans.), *Standard edition of the complete psychological works of Sigmund Freud* (Vol. 19, 243–58). London: Hogarth Press. (Original work published 1925.)

Gallop, J. (1982). *The daughter's seduction: Feminism and psychoanalysis.* Ithaca, NY: Cornell University Press.

Gergen, K. J. (1985). The social constructionist movement in modern psychology. *American Psychologist, 40,* 266–75.

Gervasio, A. H. & Crawford, M. (1989). The social evaluation of assertion: A critique and speech act reformulation. *Psychology of Women Quarterly, 13,* 1–25.

Gilbert, L. A. (1980). Feminist therapy. In A. M. Brodsky & R. T. Hare-Mustin (Eds.), *Women and psychotherapy: An assessment of research and practice* (245–65). New York: Guilford.

Gilder, G. (1987). *Men and marriage.* Los Angeles: Pelican.

Gilligan, C. (1982). *In a different voice: Psychological theory and women's development.* Cambridge: Harvard University Press.

Goldner, V. (1987). Instrumentalism, feminism, and the limit of family therapy. *Journal of Family Psychology, 1,* 109–16.

Gough, H. G. (1964). *California psychological inventory: Manual.* Palo Alto: Consulting Psychologists Press.

Grimshaw, J. (1986). *Philosophy and feminist thinking.* Minneapolis: University of Minnesota Press.

Haavind, H. (1984). Love and power in marriage. In H. Holter (Ed.), *Patriarchy in a welfare society* (136–67). Oslo: Universitets Forlaget. Distribution in U.S.: New York: Columbia University Press.

Haley, J. (1976). *Problem-solving therapy.* San Francisco: Jossey-Bass.

Harding, S. (1986). *The science question in feminism.* Ithaca, NY: Cornell University Press.

Hare-Mustin, R. T. (1978). A feminist approach to family therapy. *Family Process, 17,* 181–94.

Hare-Mustin, R. T. (1983). An appraisal of the relationship of women and psychotherapy: 80 years after the case of Dora. *American Psychologist, 1983, 38,* 593–601.

Hare-Mustin, R. T. (1987). The problem of gender in family therapy theory. *Family Process, 26,* 15–27.

Hare-Mustin, R. T. (1988). Family change and gender differences: Implications for theory and practice. *Family Relations, 37,* 36–41.

Hare-Mustin, R. T. & Marecek, J. (1986). Autonomy and gender: Some questions for therapists. *Psychotherapy, 23,* 205–12.

Hartsock, N. C. M. (1985). *Money, sex, and power: Toward a feminist historical materialism.* Boston: Northeastern University Press.

Hathaway, S. R. & McKinley, J. C. (1943). *The Minnesota Multiphasic Personality Test.* New York: Psychological Corporation.

Heisenberg, W. (1952). *Philosophical problems of nuclear science* (F. C. Hayes, Trans.). New York: Pantheon.

Hollway, W. (1984). Gender difference and the production of subjectivity. In J. Henriques, W. Hollway, C. Urwin, C. Venn & V. Walkerdine (Eds.), *Changing the subject* (26–59). London: Methuen.

Howard, G. (1985). The role of values in the science of psychology. *American Psychologist, 40*, 255–65.

Hyde, J. S. (1981). How large are cognitive gender differences? *American Psychologist, 36*, 892–901.

Jacobson, N. S. (1983). Beyond empiricism: The politics of marital therapy. *American Journal of Family Therapy, 11* (2), 11–24.

Jameson, F. (1981). *The political unconscious: Narrative as a socially symbolic act.* Ithaca, NY: Cornell University Press.

Jordan, J. V. & Surrey, J. L. (1986). The self-in-relation: Empathy and the mother-daughter relationship. In T. Bernay & D. W. Cantor (Eds.), *The psychology of today's woman: New psychoanalytic visions* (81–104). New York: The Analytic Press.

Kagan, J. (1984). *The nature of the child.* New York: Basic Books.

Keller, E. F. (1985). *Reflections on gender and science.* New Haven: Yale University Press.

Kessler, S. J. & McKenna, W. (1978). *Gender: An ethnomethodological approach.* Chicago: University of Chicago Press.

Kuhn, T. S. (1962). *The structure of scientific revolutions.* Chicago, IL: University of Chicago Press.

Lacan, J. (1985). *Feminine sexuality* (J. Mitchell & J. Rose, Eds.; J. Rose, Trans.). New York: Norton.

Lasch, C. (1977). *Haven in a heartless world.* New York: Basic Books.

Lerner, H. G. (1983). Female dependency in context: Some theoretical and technical considerations. *American Journal of Orthopsychiatry, 53*, 697–705.

Libow, J. (1985). Gender and sex role issues as family secrets. *Journal of Strategic and Systemic Therapies, 4,*(2), 32–41.

Lipman-Blumen, J. (1984). *Gender roles and power.* Englewood Cliffs, NJ: Prentice-Hall.

Lott, B. (1985). The potential enrichment of social/personality psychology through feminist research and vice versa. *American Psychologist, 40*, 155–64.

Lott, B. (1987). *Women's lives: Themes and variations.* Belmont, CA: Brooks/Cole.

Luria, Z. (1986). A methodological critique: On "In a different voice." *Signs, 11*, 316–21.

Maccoby, E. E. & Jacklin, C. N. (1975). *The psychology of sex differences.* Stanford, CA: Stanford University Press.

MacKinnon, L. K. & Miller, D. (1987). The new epistemology and the Milan approach: Feminist and sociopolitical considerations. *Journal of Marital and Family Therapy, 13,* 139–55.

Marecek, J. & Hare-Mustin, R. T. (1987, March). *Cultural and radical feminism in therapy: Divergent views of change.* Paper presented at the meeting of the American Orthopsychiatric Association, Washington, DC.

Marecek, J. & Kravetz, D. (1977). Women and mental health: A review of feminist change efforts. *Psychiatry, 40,* 323–29.

Margolin, G., Talovic, S., Fernandez, V. & Onorato, R. (1983). Sex role considerations and behavioral marital therapy: Equal does not mean identical. *Journal of Marital and Family Therapy, 9,* 131–45.

Marshner, C. (1982). *The new traditional woman.* Washington, DC: Fress Congress Education and Research Foundation.

Mednick, M. T. (1989). On the politics of psychological constructs: Stop the bandwagon, I want to get off. *American Psychologist, 44,* 1118–23.

Merchant, C. (1980). *The death of nature: Women, ecology, and the scientific revolution.* San Francisco: Harper & Row.

Miller, J. B. (1986). *Toward a new psychology of women* (2d ed.). Boston: Beacon Press.

Mills, P. J. (1987). *Woman, nature, and psyche.* New Haven: Yale University Press.

Minuchin, S. (1974). *Families and family therapy.* Cambridge: Harvard University Press.

Morawski, J. G. (1985). The measurement of masculinity and femininity: Engendering categorical realities. *Journal of Personality, 53,* 196–223.

Morawski, J. G. (1987). The troubled quest for masculinity, femininity, and androgyny. In P. Shaver & C. Hendrick (Eds.), *Review of Social and Personality Psychology: Vol. 7. Sex and gender* (44–69). Beverly Hills: Sage.

Muehlenhard, C. L. (1983). Women's assertion and the feminine sex-role stereotype. In V. Frank & E. D. Rothblum (Eds.), *The stereotyping of women: Its effects on mental health* (153–71). New York: Springer.

Nehamas, A. (1987, 5 October). Truth and consequences: How to understand Jacques Derrida. *The New Republic,* pp. 31–36.

Newland, K. (1979). *The sisterhood of man.* New York: Norton.

Nye, F. I. (1982). *Family relationships: Rewards and costs.* Beverly Hills: Sage.

Ortner, S. B. (1974). Is female to male as nature is to culture? In M. Z.

Rosaldo & L. Lamphere (Eds.), *Women, culture, and society* (67–87). Stanford: Stanford University Press.

Park, B., & Rothbart, M. (1982). Perception of out-group homogeneity and levels of social categorization: Memory for the subordinate attributes of in-group and out-group members. *Journal of Personality and Social Psychology, 42,* 1051–68.

Parsons, T. & Bales, R. F. (1955). *Family, socialization, and interaction process.* Glencoe, IL: Free Press.

Piotrkowski, C. S. & Repetti, R. L. (1984). Dual-earner families. In B. B. Hess & M. B. Sussman (Eds.), *Women and the family: Two decades of change* (99–124). New York: Haworth Press.

Pogrebin, L. C. (1983). *Family politics: Love and power on an intimate frontier.* New York: McGraw-Hill.

Ringleheim, J. (1985). Women and the Holocaust: A reconsideration of research. *Signs, 10,* 741–61.

Rorty, R. (1979). *Philosophy and the mirror of nature.* Princeton: Princeton University Press.

Rosenberg, R. (1986). Offer of proof concerning the testimony of Dr. Rosalind Rosenberg [EEOC v. Sears, Roebuck, and Company]. *Signs, 11,* 757–66.

Rossi, A. (1984). Gender and parenthood. *American Sociological Review, 49,* 1–19.

Russ, J. (1986). Letter to the editor. *Women's Review of Books, 3* (12), 7.

Sampson, E. E. (1985). The decentralization of identity: Toward a revised concept of personal and social order. *American Psychologist, 40,* 1203–11.

Scarr, S. (1985). Constructing psychology: Making facts and fables for our times. *American Psychologist, 40,* 499–512.

Schlachet, B. C. (1984). Female role socialization: The analyst and the analysis. In C. M. Brody (Ed.), *Women therapists for working with women* (55–65). New York: Springer.

Scott, J. W. (1985, December). *Is gender a useful category of historical analysis?* Paper presented at the meeting of the American Historical Association, New York.

Segal, L. (1986). *The dream of reality: Heinz von Foerster's constructivism.* New York: Norton.

Sennett, R. (1980). *Authority.* New York: Knopf.

Shields, S. A. (1975). Functionalism, Darwinism, and the psychology of women: A study in social myth. *American Psychologist, 30,* 739–54.

Spence, D. P. (1982). *Narrative truth and historical truth.* New York: Norton.

Spence, D. P. (1987). *The Freudian metaphor: Toward a paradigm change in psychoanalysis.* New York: Norton.

Spender, D. (1984). Defining reality: A powerful tool. In C. Kramarae, M. Schulz & W. M. O'Barr (Eds.), *Language and power* (194–205). Beverly Hills: Sage.

Stacey, J. (1983). The new conservative feminism. *Feminist Studies, 9,* 559–83.

Stacey, J. & Thorne, B. (1985). The missing feminist revolution in sociology. *Social Problems, 32,* 301–16.

Strainchamps, E. (Ed.). (1974). *Rooms with no view: A woman's guide to the man's world of the media.* New York: Harper & Row.

Taggart, M. (1985). The feminist critique in epistemological perspective: Questions of context in family therapy. *Journal of Marital and Family Therapy, 11,* 113–26.

Terman, L. & Miles, C. C. (1936). *Sex and personality.* New York: McGraw-Hill.

Thorne, B. (1982). Feminist rethinking of the family: An overview. In B. Thorne & M. Yalom (Eds.), *Rethinking the family: Some feminist questions* (1–24). New York: Longmans.

Tiefer, L. (1987). Social constructionism and the study of human sexuality. In P. Shaver & C. Hendrick (Eds.), *Review of Social and Personality Psychology: Vol. 7. Sex and gender* (70–94). Beverly Hills: Sage.

Tobias, S. (1986). "In a different voice" and its implications for feminism. *Women's Studies in Indiana, 12,* (2), 1–2, 4.

Unger, R. K. (1979). Toward a redefinition of sex and gender. *American Psychologist, 34,* 1085–94.

Unger, R. K. (1983). Through the looking glass: No wonderland yet! (The reciprocal relationship between methodology and models of reality). *Psychology of Women Quarterly, 8,* 9–32.

Von Glaserfeld, E. (1984). An introduction to radical constructivism. In P. Watzlawick (Ed.), *The invented reality: Contributions to constructivism* (17–40). New York: Norton.

Wallston, B. S. (1981). What are the questions in psychology of women? A feminist approach to research. *Psychology of Women Quarterly, 5,* 597–617.

Watzlawick, P. (Ed.). (1984). *The invented reality: Contributions to constructivism.* New York: Norton.

Watzlawick, P., Weakland, J. H. & Fisch, R. (1974). *Change: Principles of problem formation and problem resolution.* New York: Norton.

Weisstein, N. (1971). Psychology constructs the female. In V. Gornick & B.

K. Moran (Eds.), *Woman in sexist society* (133–46). New York: Basic Books.

Weitzman, L. J. (1985). *The divorce revolution: The unexpected social and economic consequences for women and children in America.* New York: Free Press.

Westkott, M. (1986). Historical and developmental roots of female dependency. *Psychotherapy, 23,* 213–20.

Wilden, A. (1972). *System and structure: Essays in communication and exchange.* London: Tavistock Publications.

Wittgenstein, L. (1960). *Preliminary studies for the "Philosophical Investigations": The blue and brown books.* Oxford: Blackwell.

Wittgenstein, L. (1967). *Philosophical investigations.* Oxford: Blackwell. (Original work published 1953.)

Worell, J. (1978). Sex roles and psychological well-being: Perspectives on methodology. *Journal of Consulting and Clinical Psychology, 46,* 777–91.

Worell, J. (1988). Women's satisfaction in close relationships. *Clinical Psychology Review, 8,* 477–98.

Young, I. M. (1983). Is male gender identity the cause of male domination? In J. Trebilcot (Ed.), *Mothering: Essays in feminist theory* (129–46). Totowa, NJ: Rowman & Allanheld.

3

Dual Natures or Learned Behavior

The Challenge to Feminist Psychology

BERNICE LOTT

The Challenge of Feminist Scholarship

Feminist scholarship, an integration of research and theory that has accompanied the second wave of the twentieth-century women's movement, has contributed to the enrichment and enlarged vision of the social sciences. In psychology, feminist scholars have insisted that the role played by sexist assumptions in the development of hypotheses and procedures be recognized, that research areas be expanded to include a focus on the life experiences of women, and that we study the consequences

The support and assistance I received from my Spring 1988 graduate seminar at the University of Rhode Island in clarifying and sharpening many of the ideas in this chapter are gratefully acknowledged. Thank you to Donna Caldwell, Karen Calderone, Carol Celebucki, Deborah Colagio, Jennifer Fernald, Myra Gipstein, Nancy Jackson, Diane Maluso, Cheryl Ricciardi, and Jeanette Ruth. A condensed version of this chapter was read at the conference on "Feminist Transformations of the Social Sciences," Hamilton College, Clinton, N.Y., 16 April 1988.

of patriarchy for personal development and social interaction. This feminist perspective in psychology has led to the asking of new questions; to the introduction of new concepts, models, and issues; and to an emphasis on the significance of gender in terms of its stimulus value, role prescriptions, and power correlates (e.g., Grady, 1981; Sherif, 1981; Unger, 1982).

In an article concerned with the contributions of feminist scholarship to social psychology (Lott, 1985b), I noted that the feminist presence in mainstream journals was well below what it would be if the quality of feminist work was the major criterion applied. Today, our theoretical and empirical work is being recognized and appreciated within psychology, a validation from which we can derive great pride. The raised consciousness that we have effected among our traditional colleagues can be seen in the introduction to *Sex and Gender* (Shaver & Hendrick, 1987). The editors, not themselves engaged in feminist research, begin their book by noting, "When the current wave of feminism began to break twenty-five years ago, few people anticipated one of its notable effects: the revitalization of academic disciplines as diverse as literature, history, biology, and psychology. Anticipated or not, that is surely what happened" (7).

To claim that feminist scholarship is enriching our disciplines may be too modest an assessment: Our work has served a revitalizing function. In a recent article in the *New York Times Magazine* on literary feminism (Kolbert, 1987), for example, Peter Brooks, the director of the prestigious Whitney Humanities Center at Yale University, was quoted as saying, "Anyone worth his [*sic*] salt in literary criticism today has to become something of a feminist" (110).

Feminist scholars are asking new questions, using new data, and suggesting new analyses and insights, both in women's studies programs and in traditional courses (e.g., Bronstein & Quina, 1988), which are complementary enterprises. Women's studies is where feminist scholarship is nurtured and developed, but without mainstreaming, as Catherine Stimpson (1984) has noted, "women's studies might collapse in upon itself, and speak only to itself, a closed loop" (84). By 1984, according to Stimpson, there were twenty thousand women's studies classes and five hundred separate programs in colleges across the United States, about fifty research centers, and more than twenty journals, newsletters, and presses. Such activity justifies her conclusion that "to think systematically about women and about gender is a respectable activity" (84). In psychology, 23 percent of departments surveyed in 1984–85 (Walsh, 1985) reported having at least one course on the psychology of women; and feminist psychology is flourishing in its own division within the American Psychological Association and in the more radical mother organization, the Association for Women in Psychology, which celebrated its twentieth birthday in 1989.

Gender Differences

Among the most significant and salient issues within feminist psychology is the conceptual and empirical response to the question of gender differences. One influential position emphasizes the positive consequences of women's life experiences, asserting that the imposed separateness from men and traditional responsibilities for the care of families has created a women's culture with both historical and contemporary significance. What we find if we examine women's culture carefully, according to this view, are sensitive, expressive, communal persons concerned with relationships, the needs of others, interpersonal responsibility and social harmony—persons whose primary social experiences are rooted in attachment. Women, it is said, are distinguishable from men by their unique experiences, person-oriented values, and different voice.

Thus, Carol Gilligan (1977; 1979; 1982) has rightly objected to the presentation of a general theory about moral decision making based on constructs influenced by a focus on men. She has gone on to argue that moral development in women takes a different path and results in a different perspective. She asserts that for men, justice is likely to be defined abstractly by the balancing of individual and competing rights, but that for women, moral judgments stem from interpersonal connections and are therefore likely to be influenced by considerations of care, responsibility for others, and the personal-social context. Similarly, it has been proposed (Belenky, Clinchy, Goldberger & Tarule, 1986) that women learn and gain knowledge differently from men, that women require confirmation of ability as a prerequisite for cognitive development, that they learn best in collaborative groups and in situations that provide opportunities for experiential learning, and that they prefer personal experience to abstractions.

In explaining such proposed differences between women and men, Gilligan (1986) has cautioned that these differences are "neither biologically determined nor unique" to one gender, but she makes substantial use of Nancy Chodorow's (1978) psychodynamic, object-relations analysis of early mother-child interaction, which assumes differential experiences for female and male infants with wide-ranging consequences. Chodorow maintains that where mothers are the primary caretakers of very young children, female infants are treated in ways that contribute to the experience of connectedness and identification with the mother, while male infants are treated in ways conducive to the experience of separation. It is this early experience that is postulated to provide each gender with its supposed characteristic orientation to the world and to other persons—connectedness for women, and autonomy for men—orientations that continue to be reinforced by later cultural prescriptions. Women and men, then, are said to differ fundamentally in basic personality as a result of crucial and continuing differences in socialization, beginning in infancy. This view requires that we look at adult behavior as rooted in intrapsychic factors that have produced enduring traits that are expressed more or less consistently across situations.

Positive implications for women have been drawn from this approach. Gilligan and others, notably Jean Baker Miller (1986), have urged us to recognize the strengths inherent in such attributes as sensitivity to feelings and concern for the well-being of others. This emphasis has served to empower women by encouraging us to value experiences and skills associated with women's traditional role and to appreciate women's affirmative, creative contributions to private life and potential contributions to all spheres of social endeavor. Thus, for example, Sara Ruddick (1987) has proposed that from women's practice as peacemaker, facilitator, moderator, care-giver and sympathizer comes an affinity for living cooperatively and resolving conflicts peaceably, whether these conflicts are within families, between groups, or among nations. Similar positive outcomes from women's special experiences have been proposed by others; for example, Nancy Goldberger and her colleagues (1987) suggest that what we all can learn "by listening to the woman's voice" (225) is the value for all human development of personal and collaborative experiences, of sharing and listening, and of providing confirmation of worthiness.

Adherence to the proposition that there are womanly and manly attributes, or distinctive and representative gender voices, raises many critical questions and has serious and widespread consequences for persons, politics, psychological theory and practice, and social policies. The assumption that the roots of gender socialization are so deep and strong that their effects are permanently fixed implies, as Martha Mednick (1989) has pointed out, that the outcomes are very hard to change and the burden is on the individual. Similarly, Jill Morawski (1987) cautions that psychological models of gender that view actions as the result of individual, stable, and identifiable characteristics locate barriers to achievement or personal development "largely within the individual," reify commonplace ideas about separate spheres, and do not encourage serious examination of "the processes that confirm and sustain gender." When some average differences between the way that some samples of women and men respond to some situations are "presumed to reflect the presence of some fixed attribute" of gender, as Stephanie Shields (1987) has noted, "issues regarding how those differences are moderated fall into the background" (232). If average differences between some women and men are attributed to the persons rather than to the differential experiences that are correlated with them, then gender is seen as the cause of behavior, and description is confused with explanation. Trait theories lead to such tautological conclusions as "Alice is a caring person because she is a woman." But the vital question for psychologists is how one becomes a caring person.

The focus on gender differences reinforces linguistic-cognitive habits that have predictable outcomes. Dividing human characteristics along gender lines that are linked to such dichotomies as communal vs. agentic, expressive vs. instrumental, social-emotional vs. objective-logical, or a care vs. a justice perspective provides a lens through which we view our own and others' behavior and a set for evaluation that obscures complexity and distorts experience; for example, psychological tests purporting to assess masculinity and femininity as sex-role orientations will yield a high score on masculinity for a woman who says of herself that she is self-reliant, assertive, independent, ambitious, and task-oriented (and a high score on femininity for a man who describes himself as sympathetic, warm, and expressive). But we know very well that these are *human* characteristics, manifested to varying degrees in differing circumstances by both women and men. Similarly, certain patterns of verbal interaction that have sometimes been found more commonly manifested by women than men have been identified as the "female register" or as "women's language" (cf. Aries, 1987). Not surprisingly, this woman-identified pattern is said to be characterized by "speech forms that are indicative of hesitancy, uncertainty, deference, and imprecision" (Aries, 1987, 155) or "to indicate involvement and connection in conversation and [ways] to facilitate conversations by soliciting responses from listeners" (Aries, 1987, 157). If certain ways of speaking are found to facilitate conversation and to encourage responses from others, what do we gain by labeling such a pattern as feminine and then expecting that women's verbal behavior will conform to it?

A set for gender dichotomies is likely to lead observers to interpret the same behavior differently, depending on the gender of the actor. Thus, for example, a study by Bradley (cf. Aries, 1987) found that women who used tag questions and disclaimers or who advanced arguments without support were judged to be less intelligent and knowledgeable than men who behaved the same way. Dividing human characteristics along gender lines is also likely to increase the attention we pay to particular behaviors manifested by women or men and the possibility of exaggerated or selective judgments. Newcome and Arnkoff (cf. Aries, 1987) found that women speakers were judged as having used more tag questions than men despite the objective fact that the frequency of this behavior was equal for both genders. Stephanie Shields (1987) has reported support for the hypothesis that "observers may be more likely to look for and explicitly note the presence or absence of emotional qualities in women's behavior than in men's behavior" (247). One test of this proposition involved examining references to emotion made by television news commentators immediately after the debate between the 1984 vice-presidential candidates Geraldine Ferraro and George Bush. Shields found from an examination of all references to emotion in the transcripts provided by the three commercial networks and PBS "nearly twice as many references to Ferraro's emotion [both its presence and absence] as to Bush's" (244).

To label some social behaviors as feminine, or in women's domain, and others as masculine, or in men's domain, because our culture attempts to teach them primarily to one gender while inhibiting their expression in persons of the other gender, obscures the essential human quality of the behaviors and the capacity of any person to learn virtually any response under the appropriate conditions. The linguistic-cognitive set that accompanies a focus on distinctive attributes for women and men also diminishes our appreciation of behavioral complexity. Would we, for example, judge the help given to a lost and frightened child as evidence of caring and communality when the helper is a woman but as evidence of instrumentality when the helper is a man? We know that an act of assistance can reflect a number of different characteristics or serve multiple goals in persons of either gender. Helping another person can reflect empathy and caring and, at the same time, reflect self-assurance and be self-serving (e.g., esteem enhancing).

Finally, a focus on gender differences narrows the range of possible outcomes that are proposed for certain gender-related experiences; for example, women's traditional role in the family, for which girls are typically socialized and which most women eventually practice, is said to be related to the development of nurturance, caring, sensitivity, expressiveness, and connectedness. Not attended to, however, are other probable and significant behaviors learned in this role, namely, effective problem solving, management skills, task-persistence, initiative, and so on. Which of these components of mothering do we highlight as women's strengths and identify as key features of women's different voice?

Within-Gender Variability

The careful observation and scholarship of feminists have resulted in the recognition by social scientists that women's behavior, now and in earlier times, in our own and in other cultures, does not invariably fulfill cultural expectations of femininity. These psychologists who developed measures of androgyny, for example, did so because individual differences within genders and wide overlap between women and men on most self-reported and observed behaviors strongly suggested that femininity and masculinity were not mutually exclusive, opposite poles on a single continuum. Despite such evidence, androgyny researchers continued to label some attributes as feminine and others as masculine, thus implying the existence of separate constellations of traits differentially associated with women and men. Even early data from androgyny research cast doubt on this assumption but went largely unrecognized; for example, on the *Personal Attributes Questionnaire*, in most samples (from varied backgrounds) over 40 percent of men score above the median in femininity and over 40 percent of women score above the median in masculinity (Spence & Helmreich, 1978). It is these persons who are categorized as androgynous or cross-sex typed. Scoring above the median means that one has a higher score than half of all persons tested in a particular sample. It is clear, then, that there is substantial overlap between women and men on attributes said to define femininity and masculinity.

Such data seriously challenge a separate domains approach to gender, even on the level of self-reported attributes that are likely to be considerably influenced by cultural stereotypes. We know that human behavior depends not on sex but on opportunities for practice, situational demands, anticipated and obtained consequences—variables that sometimes differentially distinguish the experiences of girls and boys, women and men, but sometimes do not. To best understand gender we must study within-gender variability as well as gender differences by investigating relationships between social behaviors and particular situational and background variables. When a society such as our own, which emphasizes gender distinctiveness, arranges social conditions to maximize separation between girls and boys and between women and men, the result is gender-related differences in expectations and practiced responses. Life conditions, however, also reflect important individual differences in personal circumstances, social class, race-ethnicity, and other social factors to which highly teachable human beings are responsive.

There is growing recognition among feminist scholars in general, and feminist psychologists in particular, that we must pay more than lip service to this general proposition. Judith Worell (1981), for example, has recently concluded that "the press of environmental and historical events and their demonstrated power to change the course of sex-role behaviors, denies the exclusive applicability of theories that rely primarily on internal variables, such as cognitive structure or personality organization. . . . [S]ex-role behaviors are not fixed in people, time, or situations but are potentially in flux" (327f). Similarly, philosopher Sandra Harding, who has previously focused on aspects of human experience that tend to separate the genders (1981), now emphasizes the variations among women, arguing that research in the biological and social sciences supports a conclusion of "plasticity rather than . . . rigidity" (1986, 661). Michelle Fine (1985), in a review of papers that appeared in the *Psychology of Women Quarterly* between 1978 and 1981, concluded that "we need to document the diversity of women's experiences . . . across categories of social class and ethnicity/race" (179). These variables, she argues, "dramatically interact with gender . . . to affect economic, social, and psychological differences among women" (180). Thus, among the criteria Hannah Lerman (1986) has suggested for a "woman-based theory of personality" is the provision for "the inclusion of the broad array of female subgroups and issues that make up the female experience" (7).

Among contemporary women in our society there are many whose experiences reinforce and maintain behavior considerably different from the traditional model. The complexity of modern society contributes to the existence of numerous subcultures and disparate models and pressures. Many women are active, independent, risk taking, competitive, or task-oriented in some contexts or across many situations. African-American women, for example, have not been expected to fit the dominant culture's stereotype of femininity, and the conditions of life for a large percentage of them have not been the same as those for most white women, just as the conditions of life for the poor are different from those for the affluent. As Bonnie Thornton Dill (1979) has pointed out, African-American women were brought as slaves to this country "to work and to produce workers," a role that contrasts sharply with domesticity and dependency. Alice Brown-Collins and Deborah Sussewell (1985) have argued that the behavior of African-American women must be understood in the context of their history and in their role as educators and community organizers as well as mothers and sisters. They note that "The irony of slave women's history is that womanhood was redefined to allow for the exploitation of their labor, resulting in the development of independent, self-reliant characteristics" (7).

When studies of gender differences include African-Americans, which is rare, interesting results are obtained. Kathryn Adams (1980), for example, paired a white or black college student with a confederate of the same or different gender and of the same or different ethnic group and had the confederates challenge picture preferences expressed by their partners. Adams assessed the degree to which the naive partners resisted changing their responses in the direction of the confederates and found that the white women were more easily influenced than the white men, but that the black women were less easily influenced than the black men, the white men, or the white women. In an earlier study, Albert Lott and I (1963) found that among a large sample of high school seniors, black girls and boys were more alike in their values and goals than white girls and boys. This was primarily a result of differences between the two groups of girls, as the white girls expressed more traditional interests and aspirations stereotypically identified with femininity. More recently, Carol Stack (1986) has reported finding more gender similarities than differences in motives and concerns among African-American migrants to the rural South. According to Stack, these women and men conceptualize their moral dilemmas in the same terms, and they "describe with force and conviction the strength of their kinship ties to their rural southern families and the nature of these ties that bind" (323).

Gender Differences in the Service of Gender Inequality

Asserting the theoretical and practical significance of within-gender variability does not deny that women (and men) in common historical-cultural circumstances share a set of experiences that shape the direction of their lives. There is little doubt, for example, that a major variable that distinguishes the adult lives of most women and men in our society is power—that is, access to, and control of, resources. As Jill Morawski (1987) has noted, "gender is not simply related to social power, it is constitutive of power relations and is a stable component in social hierarchies of power" (58). This is a conclusion that is shared by all feminist scholars regardless of theoretical differences with respect to how power inequities operate to influence gender. Thus Nancy Chodorow (1979), too, has written: "We can only understand gender difference . . . relationally and situationally, as part of a system of asymmetrical social relationships embedded in inequalities of power" (63).

Gender socialization (or sex typing) and differences in power between women and men are interrelated: Socialization describes how we learn to behave as our culture expects us to, and power differences make differential socialization necessary. Differences in power are then perpetuated and reinforced by the results of differential learning. To break this circularity we must understand how power differences between groups are related to economic, political, and other conditions and how they change the institutionalized gender differences in these conditions. As Nona Glazer (1987) has argued, for example, "all individuals have the potential to be creative, loving, cooperative, and altruistic but . . . these potentials [may be] distorted and denied them by the oppressive conditions in which they live" (298f).

An illustrative analysis is provided by Rachel Hare-Mustin and Jeanne Marecek (1986), who have argued that whether an individual's behavior reflects "autonomy or relatedness may depend more on . . . position in the social hierarchy than on gender" (209). Research by Alice Eagly and her colleagues (Eagly, 1983; Eagly & Wood, 1982) has provided a number of empirical demonstrations of this proposition and has shown that responses to women and men are based on assumptions that they occupy lower and higher positions, respectively, in a hierarchical social structure. But beyond this, Hare-Mustin and Marecek, taking off from a 1972 paper by Zuk, point out that persons in power tend to "advocate rules and rationality, while those with less power espouse relatedness and compassion." Autonomy and relatedness, then, "are transactional," and which mode a person expresses "reflects his or her relative power and status." Attaining autonomy or relatedness "is less a matter of individual accomplishment [or gender] than the result of one's location in [the] social structure" (209). Thus, autonomy, self-sufficiency, separateness, pursuit of self-interest, competence, and power—attributes that our society identifies with masculinity—as well as dependence, connectedness, and concern for others—attributes that we ascribe to femininity—are responses to situations that reflect social position and access to resources.

Recognition of the role played by differential power in the cultural construction of gender helps us to put empirically observed gender differences in perspective and to anticipate situations in which such differences will be maximized and others in which they will disappear. Thus, for example, Judith Worell (1988) notes that issues of power and control are always present in close relationships. Women might focus on different issues than men in a relationship in order to survive in the face of relative powerlessness. And, as N. Katherine Hayles (1986) has suggested, when

Carol Gilligan wrote about women's different voice as being one that emphasizes responsibility, caring, and connections, she may have been describing not so much women's lives as women's narratives or stories in which "women's anger must be suppressed." Hayles argues that the "only female voice . . . a male world will authorize" (24) is a voice of care and conciliation, not one that openly expresses anger, and that "Gilligan does not realize that her own voice has been distinctively shaped by the necessity to deny and disguise women's anger" (38).

What happens when women are in situations that discourage care, conciliation, mutuality and support and instead encourage anger, separateness, self-interest, or other behaviors that we tend to ascribe to men? Evelyn Keller and Helene Moglen (1987) have recently addressed this issue in an article on competitive behavior among academic women—behavior that contradicts the mythology of sisterhood. They attribute women's competitive behavior to new situations, an analysis that represents a sharp departure for Keller from her earlier thinking about feminine and masculine modes of doing science (1982; 1983), which she traced to gender-related experiences beginning in infancy. In the paper with Moglen, Keller now recognizes the ease with which such modes can change, and that much of the behavior commonly attributed to women is a function of women's usual position as outsiders. As this position changes, as it has for some women in academe who are now within reach of such conventional rewards as grants, prestigious jobs, and peer recognition, academic women will, according to Moglen and Keller, lose their "innocence and purity." In academe, where resources are perceived as scarce, the situation encourages competitiveness among persons of both genders.

The Empirical Fragility of Gender Differences

The characteristics of situations affect behavior in predictable ways. Thus, some women who are no longer outsiders in academe will respond to its contingencies and demands in ways similar to those of some men. This suggests that a dualistic approach to gender and a polarized view of human behavior is inadequate for understanding the complex reactions people make to complex conditions. Female domain-male domain arguments do not fare well when tested against observation of the behavior of adult women and men in diverse situations. According to Jill Morawski (1987), after decades of research the search for reliable sex differences reached an impasse in the early part of this century. She concluded that "these early studies of psychological attributes and conduct indicated that sex differences were either nonexistent, relatively insubstantial, or erratic in their patterns. . . . By the 1920s the effort to attain scientific knowledge of the psychology of gender faltered, caught in a web of inconsistent and inconclusive findings. . . . The myriad experiments yielded no discernible sex-related patterns in performance or cognition" (p. 46).

Contemporary research also supports the conclusion that behavior has no gender. There are certainly individual differences in the capacity for learning of different behaviors, but such differences have not been shown to reliably distinguish women from men. Thus, we can expect that a person of either gender can learn virtually any behavior under conditions appropriate for its acquisition, and the behavior will be maintained if it continues to effectively elicit positive consequences. To understand how culture constructs gender, as well as the distribution of behavioral variations, requires studying the factors that influence the acquisition and maintenance of behavior under differing conditions. Data from many sources support the thesis that women are found throughout the spectrum of behavioral possibilities (Lott, 1987). Culture can override individual circumstances and reinforce similar ways of behaving, producing common themes associated with gender. Variations among women (and men) are also found on every behavioral continuum. Instrumental, expressive, dominant, affiliative, autonomous, self-oriented, or communual-oriented responses are teachable and, under the appropriate conditions, can be learned, maintained, and manifested by girls or boys, women or men.

It is important to emphasize that the present analysis does not deny the potential contribution to behavior of structural or physiological characteristics, such as those associated with sex—human femaleness or maleness. John Money (1972) has concluded that there are four biological imperatives that can be related to human sex—menstruation, gestation, and lactation for females and impregnation for males. Just how these sexual distinctions interact with cultural conditions to affect the construction of gender is a vital area for study. We may find some sex-specific behaviors that are not entirely arbitrary. But we already know that among human females, for example, a sizable number who have the capacity for gestation and lactation choose not to experience them, and that menstruation is subject to environmental variation.

Among the influential contributors to the recent literature on assessment of femininity and masculinity, some have now concluded that their tests do not, in fact, measure sex-role orientations but simply personality attributes that are conceptually independent of gender. Janet Spence (1983), for example, urges investigators to interpret results from instruments presumably assessing masculinity and femininity "far more narrowly and conservatively . . . [and] only as measures of particular trait clusters" (441, 442). One cluster is identified by dominance, self-assertiveness, independence, instrumentality, and decisiveness; another by warmth, expressiveness, interpersonal orientation, and sensitivity to others. Since these clusters have been found to have only weak associations with other attributes presumed to distinguish between the genders, Spence has recommended the rejection of labels such as masculine and feminine for scales measuring traits in favor of labels "that are more descriptive of their actual content" (442). In another article Spence (1985) noted that few persons of either gender exhibit most of the qualities and behaviors stereotypically expected of them and that variables contributing to the development of sex-typed characteristics are not necessarily associated with general societal gender standards. Sandra Bem (1985), too, has reconsidered the concept of androgyny and found it problematic because "it continues to presuppose . . . that the concepts of 'femininity' and 'masculinity' have an independent and palpable reality rather than themselves being cognitive constructs"; she urges that "human behaviors and personality attributes should no longer be linked with gender" (222).

A general conclusion reached by a number of reviewers of the literature on gender differences in social behavior is that such differences are maintained by differences in status and role, that is, by relative social position and behavior relevant or appropriate to it. Alice Eagly (1987), for example, has proposed that while sex differences may have "interesting developmental histories . . . , understanding development does not necessarily enlighten us about the factors that maintain a sex difference among adults" (7). She argues that "the contemporaneous influences arising from adult social roles . . . [are] the proximal predictors of adult sex differences" (9). In support of this position, Eagly has presented quantitative and qualitative reviews of the literature on gender differences in several areas (e.g., helping, aggression, influenceability). According to her social-role analysis, sex differences in social behavior are a result of conformity to gender expectations, differential skills, and beliefs acquired as a result of prior gender-related experiences and gender differences in power. Her analyses have revealed wide inconsistencies across studies in the magnitude of gender differences, and they support her general hypotheses that such differences are more likely "to occur in settings in which gender roles are relatively more salient than any competing role expectations with counterstereotypic impact" (126). Where gender is less salient, according to this analysis, individuals will behave in ways appropriate to other social roles. "For the most part," Eagly notes, "women and men who are incumbents of the same specific roles have had many of the same prior experiences, and consequently may differ little in role-relevant skills and attitudes" (145). To roles associated with occupation and age, discussed by Eagly, we should add those associated with social class, ethnicity, minority status, and so on.

Many investigators have demonstrated that adults in similar social positions or circumstances behave similarly regardless of gender. Jerome Adams (1984), for example, studied West Point cadets in the first three coaducational classes and found no reliable gender differences in self-reported educational aspirations, professional career goals, or instrumental, assertive, and agentic personal attributes. Among advanced cadets who served as leaders during basic training, no differences were found between women and men in assessments of success or relevant behavior (Rice, Instone & Adams, 1984). Dobbins and Platz (1986) concluded from a quantitative meta-analysis of the literature on gender differences in leadership that field studies in real organizational settings have found women and men to be similar on measures of leader-relevant behaviors and to have equally satisfied subordinates. These investigators end their report by calling for "a moratorium on research that simply compares male and female leaders"; they urge, instead, investigation of the processes through which sex stereotypes lead to evaluation bias.

In a study of negotiating behavior (Pruitt, Carnevale, Forcey & Van Slyck, 1986) in which members of same-gender pairs were instructed to play the roles of buyer and seller under various conditions, women and men were found not to differ in negotiating behavior. Another group of investigators (Reis, Senchak & Solomon, 1985), concerned with intimacy in social interaction, found that when a sample of college women and men were asked to have an intimate conversation with their best friend, there were no gender differences in meaningfulness or intimacy as assessed by either external judges or self-ratings. The investigators concluded that intimacy differences between the genders are not immutable, and that men are as capable as women of interacting intimately "when the situation makes it desirable to do so" (1215). Relevant to this conclusion is one reached by Judith Worell (1988) from a review of research on support and satisfaction in close relationships. Many of these studies, she notes, have found that gender takes a back seat to individual differences in such attributes as warmth, interpersonal skills, nurturance, and self-disclosure. She concluded that "gender dichotomies are less useful in understanding intimate interactions than are the specific needs, motives, intentions, and skills that each partner brings to the dyad" (492).

Brenda Major (1987) has argued that when women reward themselves less than men for objectively equivalent performance, and express as much satisfaction with their jobs and pay as men despite objective inequities in job-related rewards, it is not because women and men have different values, but because women have a lower sense of entitlement. This sense of entitlement is derived, according to Major, from the fact that women compare their outcomes with those that they have received in the past, or with those received by persons similar to themselves in gender and employment category, and expect their work to be devalued. A woman's low sense of entitlement is thus supported by objective data: "women typically are paid less than men, and people working in female-dominated jobs are paid less that those working in male dominated jobs" (Major, 1987, 132). Products, performance, and credentials attributed to a woman are typically judged more negatively than the identical products, performance, and credentials attributed to a man (Lott, 1985a). Under conditions in which women compare themselves to other social groups, however, gender differences disappear. In one study by Major and her colleagues, for example, when students who were working on a sex-neutral task were provided with social comparison information about what previous participants had paid themselves for the same task, "no gender differences in self-pay were observed. . . . Women and men . . . paid themselves approximately the average amount taken by . . . [the previous participants], regardless of sex" (Major, 1987, 134). In another study, students were assigned to work on an identical task, but for some it was labeled feminine and for others masculine or sex-neutral. It was found that regardless of gender, those assigned to the feminine-labeled job expected to earn less pay for it and subsequently judged that the pay they received was more fair than did persons assigned to the "masculine" job.

Even more convincing evidence of the fragility of gender differences in reward allocations or job expectations under conditions in which other social roles or situational demands are more salient are findings from studies of employed adults. In an important study of a large and heterogeneous sample, Faye Crosby (1982) found that women and men in high-prestige jobs were very similar in their answers to questions about the sources of gratification in their work, citing the same factors: pay, interpersonal relationships, and the desire for independence and control. In another study (Golding, Resnick & Crosby, 1983), women and men lawyers were interviewed and found to express no reliable differences in job values, work-related gratifications, or work-related problems. Some value differences were found, however, between lawyers and secretaries. Similarly, an investigation of blue-collar steel workers by Deaux and Ullman found that "men and women were alike in their self-evaluations, their aspirations, and their likes and dislikes about the work situation" (Deaux, 1984, 114). While jobs and pay outcomes are often associated with gender, these are not unchangeable or inevitable. To raise women's current sense of entitlement, then, as Major (1987) has concluded, requires elevating the outcomes for those with whom women compare themselves and recognizing "the influence of unjustifiable procedures on current reward structures" (145).

The frequent confounding of gender with status has also been identified by Elizabeth Aries (1987) in the literature on gender and communication. Many studies, she notes, have demonstrated "gender differences in the patterning of both verbal and nonverbal communication . . . [with men's interactions] characterized as more task-oriented, dominant, directive, hierarchical; and women's as more social-emotional, expressive, supportive, facilitative, cooperative, personal, and egalitarian" (170). But these gender differences, she cautions, "must not be overdrawn, . . . are not absolute across situations, and are greatly reduced or even reversed in some contexts" (170). In a study of her own, for example, of a group of women and men described as bright, career-oriented, and with similar scores on measures of dominance and other personal attributes, she found that women contributed more to interaction than men in six out of eight mixed-gender group discussions. Similarly, a study by Hersley and Werner (cf. Aries, 1987) found that in couples "where wives were active in the women's liberation movement, wives spoke longer than husbands, whereas husbands spoke longer than wives in couples where wives were not active in the movement" (158). Thus, under some circumstances and social conditions gender differences in communication are opposite to what would be predicted from stereotyped expectations. And in other situations, no reliable gender differences have been reported—for example, at an information booth or when buying a train ticket. That social status is a more significant variable than gender in influencing speech patterns is suggested by the findings of Crosby and Nyquist (cf. Aries, 1987). They found more hesitancy, imprecision, and deference in the speech of clients of both genders than in the speech of police personnel.

Gender differences have been found to vary with the situation in which they are assessed and also with the operations used to measure them; for example, a series of analyses by Eisenberg and Lennon (1983) of the research literature on empathy resulted in the conclusion that while women and men are typically found to differ on self-report measures of empathy, few gender differences are found when empathy is assessed by physiological measures of arousal or by observations of nonverbal behavior (e.g., facial expressions). Sometimes a gender-difference conclusion from one research setting is challenged by data from another setting. A recent investigation by Friedman, Robinson, and Friedman (1987), for example, focused explicitly on moral judgments and tested the hypothesis that women are more likely to resolve moral dilemmas by means of care-based considerations, while men are more likely to rely on justice-based considerations. Among a sample of college students who responded to four moral dilemmas by rating the importance of twelve different statements reflecting care and justice considerations, no reliable gender differences were found. Measures of sex-typed personality attributes also failed to predict differences in moral judgments, and "men and women showed highly similar patterns in rating the importance of individual items in each dilemma" (44).

While there is an "intuitive appeal," as Mary Brabeck (1983) has pointed out, to the claim that compassion is a quality more valued by women and that women are more compassionate than men, there is evidence that contradicts these beliefs. Historian Linda Kerber (1986), for example, has commented on the fact that women's achievement of the vote in this country failed to "usher in a new world" as had been promised by the suffragists.

> Give women the vote, the argument went, and the streets would be clean, child labor would be eliminated, war would be at an end. . . . Suffragists were right in expecting that support for peace movements and progressive legislation would come from newly enfranchised women, but they were wrong to predict that most women would support a political agenda drawn up from the concerns central to women's sphere. Newly enfranchised women voted as the interests of their race and class dictated. (P. 309)

Helena Lewis (1988), in reviewing a collection of articles (by Higonnet et al.) on women's role in the two world wars, concluded that the articles challenge "the common assumption that only men fight" in wars. Women have engaged in combat and joined guerilla or resistance movements. Women have also participated in acts of terrorism, and their substantial contributions to Nazi ideology and to practices of extermination and genocide has been documented by recent scholarship (Bridenthal, Grossman & Kaplan, 1984; Koonz, 1987). Thus real world behaviors often contradict the stereotyped expectations for women—even with respect to their presumed attachment to a morality of care.

Some investigators have stressed the importance of examining the magnitude of the gender differences in behavior or cognitive skills and have utilized quantitative methods (meta-analyses) to integrate and evaluate large numbers of studies pertaining to the same hypothesis. According to Alice Eagly (1987), who has reviewed the meta-analytical literature on gender differences, the overall percentage of variability in social behaviors that is attributable to gender is "generally below 10% and more typically 5%" (115). This means that with respect to any given measure thus far utilized, gender can explain, on the average, only about 5 to 10 percent of the variation among persons. Judith Hall (1987), who did a meta-analysis of the substantial literature on nonverbal behavior, concluded that the largest gender difference (accounting for 26 percent of the variance) was for filling in of pauses with such expressions as "er," "ah," and "um." But it is men speakers who have been found to use such pause fillers significantly more than women, a result opposite to that of stereotyped expectation.

It seems clear that a belief in enduring, deep-seated, transcendent gender differences does not fare well when tested against observations and investigations of the behavior of adult women and men in diverse situations. Reviews of the empirical literature on gender differences have typically concluded that gender by itself has relatively weak associations with behavior. The "now you see them, now you don't" quality of gender differences (Unger, 1981) is understandable because the appearance of gender differences in behavior depends on social context and particular situational conditions. As Kay Deaux (1984) concluded from her review of the literature: "Main effects of sex are frequently qualified by situational interactions, and the selection of tasks plays a critical role in eliciting or suppressing differences. Furthermore, the amount of variance accounted for by sex, even when main effects are reliable, is typically quite small. Thus, when any particular behavior is considered, [gender] differences . . . may be of relatively little consequence" (108).

Personal experiences and systematically collected data support the conclusions that human behavior is not well described by traits, that is, stable intrapsychic consistencies in behavior tendencies, and that individuals learn responses to, and in, situations continuously throughout our lives. As conditions and opportunities for practice change, so does our behavior. There is thus good reason to question the validity of theories that assume gender polarities and support a dualistic vision of human functioning. It is important to examine carefully the consequences of such a position for personal growth, for politics, and for psychological theory and practice.

Consequences of a Dual Natures Construction of Gender

Despite contrary evidence, we seem to be drawn to theories that ignore complexities and syntheses in favor of dualities. As noted by Londa Schiebinger (1987):

The basic categories of modern thought have . . . taken shape as a series of dualities: reason has been opposed to feeling, fact to value, culture to nature, science to belief, the public to the private. . . . When the dualism of masculinity and femininity was mapped onto these categories, masculinity became synonymous with reason and objectivity— qualities associated with participation in public spheres of government, commerce, science, and scholarship. Femininity became synonymous with feeling and subjectivity— qualities associated with the private sphere of hearth and home. (330f)

Careful examination of these conceptual dichotomies has led many to conclude that they lack empirical support. Jill Morawski (1987), for example, refers to these dualisms as having "dubious heritages and a paucity of empirical warrant" (60).

Although the picture of the cooperative, caring, person-oriented adult woman drawn by the newer proponents of a feminine-masculine dichotomy is different from, and more positive than, the earlier negative portraits associated with Freud or Erikson, both visions have in common a focus on traits, stable personality components that are presumed to predispose to particular ways of behaving across situations. Both the older psychoanalytic and the newer female domain positions also ascribe to infancy an all-important role in shaping personality, and both see different sets of characteristics as likely outcomes for each gender. As historian Linda Kerber (1986) has pointed out, Gilligan's formulations, for example, "suggest that what was once called a separate sphere . . . was in fact a personality called into existence by women's distinctive psychological development" (307). And while Chodorow (1978) asserts that different gender outcomes should follow from different parenting arrangements, gender differences are attributed fundamentally to caregiver-infant relationships in the earliest period of development. These views, in general, seem to reflect a culturally limited perspective—that of middle-class white nuclear families. To use the historically recent family structure of industrialized, Western societies as a model from which to draw conclusions about mother-child relationships and human personality is to make the same kind of mistake feminists have identified in traditional social science—that of using man as the prototype of a human being.

So seemingly irresistible is the notion of polarized and opposed gender attributes, however, that it continues to occupy a salient position in the work of social scientists, in mainstream culture, and in the formulation of social policy. I have chosen two examples to illustrate this. I first examine an article by Francesca

Cancian (1986), "The Feminization of Love." Her thesis is that the conception of love prevalent in social science and the popular media identified it with emotional expression, emotional closeness, and verbal self-disclosure, while instrumental and physical aspects such as helping or sharing in activities and having sex, are ignored. She argues persuasively that both expressive and instrumental behaviors are part of a loving relationship and that men as well as women are capable of love and of manifesting it. She cites research showing that when behaviors rather than attitudes are measured, men and women are found to be similar in expressions of love. Nevertheless, Cancian's own choice of language ties her to a dualistic view of gender, and she persists in identifying two styles of love—emotional closeness-verbal self-disclosure (the feminine), and instrumental help-sex (the masculine). She dichotomizes styles of love despite providing illustrations of their interrelationship. She notes, for example, that "in reality, a major way by which women are loving is in the clearly instrumental activities associated with caring for others" (706f). She is critical of those feminist scholars who "reinforce the distinction between feminine expressiveness and masculine instrumentality," asserting that such a false distinction will "revive the ideology of separate spheres, and legitimate the popular idea that only women know the right way to love" (708). Yet her own distinction between masculine and feminine styles of love is subject to the same criticism. She advocates an "androgynous perspective" while pointing out in a footnote that the concept of "'androgyny' is problematic" in that "it assumes rather than questions sex-role stereotypes." But this is the approach she chooses to use.

In an earlier paper (Lott, 1981) I argued that while the concept of androgyny was an advance over the earlier idea of masculine and feminine as bipolar opposites because it validated the behavior of persons with wide and flexible behavioral repertoires, androgyny continues to link behavior to gender by labeling certain attributes as characteristic of women (i.e., feminine) and others as characteristic of men (i.e., masculine). I said then that "to label some behaviors as feminine and some as masculine, as androgyny researchers do, and then to put the two artificial pieces back together again* to conform with the reality of human functioning and capability (and to suggest that the 'whole' is preferable to the parts . . .) is to reinforce verbal habits which undermine the possibility of degenderizing behavior" (178).

The popularity of the androgyny model has not altered the ubiquitousness of the dualistic approach to gender or the serious social consequences that follow from adherence to it. This can be illustrated by the recent federal court decision in the case of the federal Equal Employment Opportunities Commission (EEOC) v. Sears, Roebuck and Company. Acting under the provisions of the Civil Rights Act of 1964, the EEOC urged America's large corporations to adopt affirmative action plans and submit them for review. In a brief history of the Sears case, Sandi Cooper (1986) described what happened: After years of dialogue and effort, EEOC concluded in 1979 "that the Sears plan had made little difference in the salaries and status of women employees" (753). EEOC proceeded to file suit against Sears "charging discrimination in two main categories of employment: commission sales—the selling of items with high ticket prices that netted high commissions . . . ; and wage differences between men and women in managerial and administrative jobs" (754). To demonstrate a pattern of discrimination, EEOC presented statistics on numbers of women who applied for jobs, who were hired, and the types of jobs they were offered. Sears countered by arguing that it had not discriminated against women but that women simply avoid competitive and threatening jobs and differ in this respect from

---

*Footnote from Lott, 1981, 178: I am indebted to Arnold Kahn for the Humpty-Dumpty analogy. He suggested it during discussion of a paper I presented at a conference of the Association for Women in Psychology in Santa Monica, California, in August 1980.

men. In February 1986, Judge Nordberg of the Northern Illinois U.S. District Court "ruled that the EEOC had not proven its charges" (756), noting that his ruling had been heavily influenced by the testimony of a noted expert in women's history, Rosalind Rosenberg of Barnard College.

Rosenberg had testified for Sears that "women's participation in the labor force is affected by the values they have internalized" (1986, 763). What are these values? Women, said Rosenberg, are "more relationship-centered" than men, "derive their self-image from their role as wife and mother [and] tend to be more interested than men in the cooperative, social aspects of the work situation" (763). Those who choose "jobs typically pursued by men often experience doubts about their ability to do well" (764), and women, in general, are less competitive, less aggressive and less able to behave as leaders than men largely because they have not had men's "extensive experience in competitive sports" (765). The judge liked this argument and interpreted the evidence provided by EEOC as being more indicative of women's avoidance of certain jobs than of a pattern of discrimination by Sears. A contrary argument presented by Alice Kessler-Harris, professor of history from Hofstra University, who testified for the EEOC did not persuade the judge. Kessler-Harris's major thesis was that in all periods of history, "substantial numbers of women have been available for jobs at good pay in whatever field those jobs are offered, and no matter what the hours" (1986, 779), and that the record of women's job performance belies the myth that there are some jobs for which women are not suited.

It is not surprising that the separate spheres argument was the one that impressed the judge in the Sears case. As Rachel Hare-Mustin (1987) has noted, there has always been a "ready acceptance" of gender differences "because these ideas preserve the status quo and do not demand that either society or individuals change" (23); instead they "serve to maintain a social system based on [differential] power" (24). The Sears case illustrates this conclusion only too well. It also illustrates the inseparability of science from its cultural context and the mutual, interactive influence of each on the other. Kenneth Gergen (1988) has urged us to understand that "scientists do not serve as passionless automatons steeped in the rigors of holding mirrors to reality. Rather, in the very formulation of problems, the choice of possible solutions, and the attempt to evaluate one solution against the other, they are already entering into the life of the culture" (20).

Nina Baym (1988), in reviewing Nancy Cott's history of the women's movement in the United States in the early part of this century, notes that contemporary feminism faces many of same divisive issues that were present earlier, particularly the distinction between "a consensus view of women's nature" and the awareness of "women's diversity." Baym argues that in the 1920s, "inevitably . . . every formulation of the interests that women are supposed to share, every account of the traits that women presumably possess in common, tended to affirm patronizing views of women's capacities and proper place. Feminists claiming a group identity for women slipped into nostalgic and damaging stereotypes" (15). The Sears case illustrates this inevitability only too well.

Gender: Learned Behavior and Stimulus Functions

A careful look at the accumulated relevant research on gender indicates that differences between women and men or between girls and boys can reliably be found for some behaviors, at some ages, in some situations, at some times and places. But such differences are better understood if related to their antecedents and situational determinants than if simply related to sex. A conceptualization of human capacities, inclinations, and behavior in terms of gender dichotomies obscures the complexities of women's (and men's) experiences, serves to generate and perpetuate gender-related differences, and diverts our attention from formulating the more significant questions for psychological research. If a culture arranges the experiences of its children and adults so that gender will be associated with differential expectations, opportunities, and consequences, it is those arrangements that we must study in order to understand their outcomes for behavior. If we want to understand and explain nurturance or empathy, assertiveness or achievement motivation, or varying orientations in the solution of moral dilemmas, then we should focus on the behavior we are concerned with and search for probable antecedents in persons of both genders.

An example of this kind of research is a study of empathy by Barnett, Howard, King, and Dino (1980). These investigators found that in a sample of college students, women scored reliably higher than men on a self-report measure of empathy, but that high empathy persons of both genders, compared with low empathy persons of both genders, similarly reported that their parents had spent more time with them, been more affectionate with them, and more often discussed feelings. With respect to these variables, women reported more than men that their mothers had discussed feelings with them and that their parents had displayed affection toward them. Thus, the same experiences appear to enhance empathy in both genders, but these experiences were reported as present more often for girls than for boys. A similar approach has been taken by Melson and Fogel (1988) with respect to nurturance. Their own research and that of others on the learning of care giving by children has led them to conclude that "boys are not less 'naturally' nurturant than girls. Until they are 4 or 5, both sexes are equally interested in babies and their care, and even after that, boys are as nurturant as girls in other ways" (45). The more practice in care giving, the more nurturance children display; differences in knowledge about the care of babies, for example, are related to age and experience, not the child's gender. In a study of parental reports of their children's behavior, no support was found for "the idea of the all-around 'caring' child" (44). One child might exhibit caring toward babies, another toward a pet animal, and another toward a younger sibling.

If we believe that readiness to exhibit a wide range of possible responses to situations contributes to effective personal functioning and group life, and that expressive, instrumental, communal, and agentic ways of behaving are acquired with practice and positive consequences, then our task as feminist psychologists is clear. Let us investigate the conditions under which persons of both genders learn to respond assertively, with compassion, and so on. An enlarged conception of morality, for example, such as has been suggested by Mary Brabeck (1983), would "ensure justice be accorded each person while maintaining a passionate concern for the well-being and care of each individual." Such a view of morality is not one that combines so-called feminine and masculine elements, but one that dispenses with such artificial dualities. Such a view focuses, instead, on the conditions that are most likely to lead to combining the value of autonomy with that of interconnection in the solution of moral-social problems.

Among the many conclusions that the data on gender differences and within-gender variability may suggest is one that I find particularly intriguing. Despite the ubiquitousness of gender associations and stereotypes, the cultural emphasis on separate spheres, and societal arrangements to maintain them, reliable gender differences turn out to be very small and unstable and their magnitude is inconsistent across situations. This suggests that persons learn wherever there are any opportunities to practice behavior, and that gender provides only one set of role expectations. Despite the powerful influence of gender stereotypes, which serve to "maintain the social order" by inducing conformity (Eagly, 1987, 134), gender typically explains no more than 5 percent of the variance in social behavior. Thus, if the objective is to explain a given social behavior such as assertiveness, or skill in decoding nonverbal cues, or resistance to group pressure, then gender, despite the influence of stereotypes and sex typing, is an inadequate predictor. The preponderant amount of variation in these behaviors—95 percent—is attributable to factors other than gender. Identification of these other variables and the magnitude of their importance is a primary task of psychologists that is impeded and sidetracked by a preoccupation with gender differences.

Feminist research in psychology should focus on the antecedents of behaviors that culture has paired with gender and, at the same time, we must include all within-gender variations in our understanding and definition of what it means to be a woman (or a man). We have impressive evidence of historical and current variations among both women and men in life-styles, aspirations, attitudes, and interests of differences between those who are affluent and those who are poor, between those who are light-skinned and people of color. But, while our research data and personal observations amply support the conclusion that no human behavior is exclusively the province of one group of persons rather than another, we must not forget that gender continues to function as a cue for position in our society, and that women and men differ widely in access to resources and to opportunities for personal growth. Gender continues to function as a central organizing principle in social institutions, to signify differences in prestige and power, and to connote differences in personal attributes. Gender labels continue to be salient stimuli to which most of us have learned similar responses.

It may well be, as Judith Lorber (1986) has suggested, that the "long-term goal of feminism must be no less than the eradication of gender as an organizing principle of postindustrial society" (568). The demand for gender equality, alone, does not challenge the separate spheres argument that perpetuates divisions in family and marketplace labor and "which in turn results in women's lesser access to control of valued resources and positions of power" (577); instead, Lorber argues, women and men must be "seen as socially interchangeable." To insist that gender not be tied to differential access to the resources of family, community, or society does not in any way suggest that certain resources should have higher value than others. And a likely outcome from the inclusion of groups with previously restricted access to resources (such as women, minorities, and the poor) is an enlarged and enriched definition of what constitutes a valuable skill or positive consequence or other ingredient of power.

REFERENCES

Adams, J. (1984). Women at West Point: A three-year perspective. *Sex Roles, 11*, 525–41.

Adams, K. A. (1980). Who has the final word? Sex, race, and dominance behavior. *Journal of Personality and Social Psychology, 38*, 1–8.

Aries, E. (1987). Gender and communication. In P. Shaver & C. Hendrick (Eds.), *Sex and gender* (149–76). Newbury Park, CA: Sage.

Barnett, M. A., Howard, J. A., King, L. M. & Dino, G. A. (1980). Antecedents of empathy: Retrospective accounts of early socialization. *Personality and Social Psychology Bulletin, 6*, 361–65.

Baym, N. (1988, January 10). What did women want? *New York Times Book Review*, 15.

Belenky, M., Clinchy, B., Goldberger, N. & Tarule, J. (1986). *Women's ways of knowing: The development of self, voice, and mind.* New York: Basic Books.

Bem, S. L. (1985). Androgyny and gender schema theory: A conceptual and empirical integration. In T. B. Sonderegger (Ed.), *Nebraska symposium on motivation 1984: Psychology and gender* (Vol. 32, 179–226). Lincoln: University of Nebraska Press.

Brabeck, M. (1983). Moral judgment: Theory and research on differences between males and females. *Developmental Review, 3*, 274–91.

Bridenthal, R., Grossman, A., & Kaplan, M. (1984). *When biology became destiny: Women in Weimar and Nazi Germany.* New York: Monthly Review Press.

Bronstein, P. & Quina, K. (1988). *Teaching a psychology of people.* Washington, DC: American Psychological Association.

Brown-Collins, A. R. & Sussewell, D. R. (1985). *Afro-American woman's emerging selves: A historical and theoretical model of self-concept.* Unpublished paper, Brown University, Providence, RI.

Cancian, F. M. (1986). The feminization of love. *Signs, 11,* 692–709.

Chodorow, N. (1978). *The reproduction of mothering: Psychoanalysis and the sociology of gender.* Berkeley: University of California Press.

Chodorow, N. (1979). Feminism and difference: Gender, relation, and difference in psychoanalytic perspective. *Socialist Review, 46,* 42–64.

Cooper, S. E. (1986). Women's history goes to trial: EEOC v. Sears, Roebuck and Company. Introduction to the documents. *Signs, 11,* 753–56.

Crosby, F. (1982). *Relative deprivation and working women.* New York: Oxford University Press.

Deaux, K. (1984). From individual differences to social categories: Analysis of a decade's research on gender. *American Psychologist, 39,* 105–16.

Dill, B. T. (1979). The dialectics of black womanhood. *Signs, 4,* 543–55.

Dobbins, G. H. & Platz, S. J. (1986). Sex differences in leadership: How real are they? *Academy of Management Review, 11,* 118–27.

Eagly, A. H. (1983). Gender and social influence: A social psychological analysis. *American Psychologist, 38,* 971–81.

Eagly, A. H. (1987). *Sex differences in social behavior: A social-role interpretation.* Hillsdale, NJ: Erlbaum.

Eagly, A. H. & Wood, W. (1982). Inferred sex differences in status as a determinant of gender stereotypes about social influence. *Journal of Personality and Social Psychology, 43,* 915–28.

Eisenberg, N. & Lennon, R. (1983). Sex differences in empathy and related capacities. *Psychological Bulletin, 94,* 100–31.

Fine, M. (1985). Reflections on a feminist psychology of women: Paradoxes and prospects. *Psychology of Women Quarterly, 9,* 167–83.

Friedman, W. J., Robinson, A. B. & Friedman, B. L. (1987). Sex differences in moral judgments? A test of Gilligan's theory. *Psychology of Women Quarterly, 11,* 37–46.

Gergen, K. J. (1988). Feminist critique of science and the challenge of social epistemology. In M. M. Gergen (Ed.), *Feminist thought and the structure of knowledge* (27–48). New York: New York University Press.

Gilligan, C. (1977). In a different voice: Women's conception of the self and of morality. *Harvard Educational Review, 47,* 481–517.

Gilligan, C. (1979). Woman's place in man's life cycle. *Harvard Educational Review, 49,* 431–46.

Gilligan, C. (1982). *In a different voice: Psychological theory and women's development.* Cambridge, MA: Harvard University Press.

Gilligan, C. (1986). Reply by Carol Gilligan. *Signs, 11,* 324–33.

Glazer, N. Y. (1987). Questioning eclectic practice in curriculum change: A Marxist perspective. *Signs, 12,* 293–304.

Goldberger, N. R., Clinchy, B. M., Belenky, M. F. & Tarule, J. M. (1987).

Women's ways of knowing: On gaining a voice. In P. Shaver & C. Hendrick (Eds.), *Sex and gender* (201–28). Newbury Park, CA: Sage.

Golding, J., Resnick, A. & Crosby, F. (1983). Work satisfaction as a function of gender and job status. *Psychology of Women Quarterly, 7*, 286–90.

Grady, K. E. (1981). Sex bias in research design. *Psychology of Women Quarterly, 5*, 628–36.

Hall, J. A. (1987). On explaining gender differences: The case of nonverbal communication. In P. Shaver & C. Hendrick (Eds.), *Sex and gender* (177–200). Newbury Park, CA: Sage.

Harding, S. (1981). What is the real material base of patriarchy and capital? In L. Sargent (Ed.), *Women and revolution* (135–63). Boston: South End Press.

Harding, S. (1986). The instability of the analytical categories of feminist theory. *Signs, 11*, 645–64.

Hare-Mustin, R. T. (1987). The problem of gender in family therapy theory. *Family Process, 26*, 15–27.

Hare-Mustin, R. T. & Marecek, J. (1986). Autonomy and gender: Some questions for therapists. *Psychotherapy, 23*, 205–12.

Hayles, N. K. (1986). Anger in different voices: Carol Gilligan and *The Mill on the Floss. Signs, 12*, 23–39.

Keller, E. F. (1982). Feminism and science. *Signs, 7*, 589–602.

Keller, E. F. (1983, September-October). Feminism as an analytic tool for the study of science. *Academe*, 15–21.

Keller, E. F. & Moglen, H. (1987). Competition and feminism: Conflicts for academic women. *Signs, 12*, 493–511.

Kerber, L. K. (1986). Some cautionary words for historians. *Signs, 11*, 304–10.

Kessler-Harris, A. (1986). Written testimony of Alice Kessler-Harris [EEOC v. Sears, Roebuck and Company]. *Signs, 11*, 767–79.

Kolbert, E. (1987, 6 December). Literary feminism comes of age. *New York Times Magazine*, 110–17.

Koonz, C. (1987). *Mothers in the fatherland: Women, family-life, and Nazi ideology. 1900–1945.* New York: St. Martin's Press.

Lerman, H. (1986). From Freud to feminist personality theory: Getting here from there. *Psychology of Women Quarterly, 10*, 1–18.

Lewis, H. (1988, January). A battlefield of one's own. *Women's Review of Books.*

Lorber, J. (1986). Dismantling Noah's ark. *Sex Roles, 14*, 567–80.

Lott, A. J. & Lott, B. E. (1963). *Negro and white youth.* New York: Holt, Rinehart & Winston.

Lott, B. (1981). A feminist critique of androgyny: Toward the elimination of gender attributions for learned behavior. In C. Mayo & N. Henley (Eds.), *Gender and nonverbal behavior* (171–80). New York: Springer.

Lott, B. (1985a). The devaluation of women's competence. *Journal of Social Issues, 41*, (4), 43–60.

Lott, B. (1985b). The potential enrichment of social/personality psychology through feminist research and vice versa. *American Psychologist, 40*, 155–64.

Lott, B. (1987). *Women's lives: Themes and variations in gender learning*. Monterey, CA: Brooks/Cole.

Major, B. (1987). Gender, justice, and the psychology of entitlement. In P. Shaver & C. Hendrick (Eds.), *Sex and gender* (124–48). Newbury Park, CA: Sage.

Miller, J. B. (1986). *Toward a new psychology of women*. Boston: Beacon.

Mednick, M. T. (1989). On the politics of psychological constructs: Stop the bandwagon, I want to get off. *American Psychologist, 44*, 1118–23.

Melson, G. F. & Fogel, A. (1988, January). Learning to care. *Psychology Today*, 39–45.

Money, J. (1972, December). *Nativism versus culturalism in gender-identity differentiation*. Paper presented at the meeting of the American Association for the Advancement of Science, Washington, DC.

Morawski, J. G. (1987). The troubled quest for masculinity, femininity, and androgyny. In P. Shaver & C. Hendrick (Eds.), *Sex and gender* (44–69). Newbury Park, CA: Sage.

Pruitt, D. G., Carnevale, P. J. D., Forcey, B. & Van Slyck, M. (1986). Gender effects in negotiation: Constituent surveillance and contentious behavior. *Journal of Experimental Social Psychology, 22*, 264–75.

Reis, H. T., Senchak, M. & Solomon, B. (1985). Sex differences in the intimacy of social interaction: Further examination of potential explanations. *Journal of Personality and Social Psychology, 48*, 1204–17.

Rice, R. W., Instone, D. & Adams, J. (1984). Leader sex, leader success, and leadership process: Two field studies. *Journal of Applied Psychology, 69*, 12–31.

Rosenberg, R. (1986). Offer of proof concerning the testimony of Dr. Rosalind Rosenberg [EEOC v. Sears, Roebuck and Company]. *Signs, 11*, 757–66.

Ruddick, S. (1987). Beyond moral theory: Political and legal implications of difference. In E. F. Kittay & D. T. Meyers (Eds.), *Women and moral theory* (237–55), Totowa, NJ: Rowman and Littlefield.

Schiebinger, L. (1987). The history and philosophy of women in science: A review essay. *Signs, 12*, 305–22.

Shaver, P. & Hendrick, C. (1987). *Sex and gender.* Newbury Park, CA: Sage.

Sherif, C. (1981). Needed concepts in the study of gender identity. *Psychology of Women Quarterly, 6,* 375–98.

Shields, S. A. (1987). Women, men, and the dilemma of emotion. In P. Shaver & C. Hendrick (Eds.), *Sex and gender* (229–50). Newbury Park, CA: Sage.

Spence, J. T. (1983). Commentary on Lubinski, Tellegen, and Butcher's "Masculinity, femininity, and androgyny viewed and assessed as distinct concepts." *Journal of Personality and Social Psychology, 44,* 440–46.

Spence, J. T. (1985). Gender identity and its implications for the concepts of masculinity and femininity. In T. B. Sonderegger (Ed.), *Nebraska symposium on motivation 1984: Psychology and gender* (Vol., 32, 59–96). Lincoln: University of Nebraska Press.

Spence, J. T. & Helmreich, R. L. (1978). *Masculinity and femininity: Their psychological dimensions, correlates, and antecedents.* Austin: University of Texas Press.

Stack, C. (1986). The culture of gender: Women and men of color. *Signs, 11,* 321–24.

Stimpson, C. R. (1984, October). What lies beyond "The Woman as Victim" construct. *Ms.,* 83–84.

Unger, R. K. (1981). Sex as a social reality: Field and laboratory research. *Psychology of Women Quarterly, 5,* 645–53.

Unger, R. K. (1982). Advocacy versus scholarship revisited: Issues in the psychology of women. *Psychology of Women Quarterly, 7,* 5–17.

Walsh, M. R. (1985). The psychology of women course: A continuing catalyst for change. *Teaching of Psychology 12,* 198–203.

Worell, J. (1981). Life-span sex roles: Development, continuity, and change. In R. N. Lerner & N. A. Busch-Rossnagel (Eds.), *Individuals as producers of their development.* New York: Academic Press.

Worell, J. (1988). Women's satisfaction in close relationships. *Clinical Psychology Review, 8,* 477–98.

4

Imperfect Reflections of Reality

Psychology Constructs Gender

RHODA K. UNGER

More than ten years ago I suggested that the matter of sex differences was something of a red herring for feminist psychologists, that is, that questions about sex differences were not *our* questions (Unger, 1979b). Such differences, however, have remained a major focus of psychologists interested in sex and gender despite numerous theoretical and methodological critiques. This chapter argues against the study of sex differences in light of recent developments in feminist theory and practice. I hope that this analysis and the others in this book will help us to understand why we keep asking questions about male-female differences and to reframe some other important questions.

Feminist Critiques of Research on Sex Differences

In the process of writing this chapter I reviewed my earlier criticisms of research on sex differences (Unger, 1979b). Most of these criticisms, unfortunately, still apply today. These criticisms (with some up-to-date interpolations) are as follows:

1. Answers to questions about sex differences are descriptive—they do not illuminate the mechanisms by which such differences are produced. Indeed, they can delay the search for mechanisms because they lead researchers to believe that biological explanations are sufficient for understanding differences in behavior between males and females. The source of this problem seems to be confusion between biological and social categories. Since males and females fit into two easily definable biological groups, it is easy to categorize them socially in terms of the same two groups. And, since biological processes have historical precedence and are often viewed as more real than social processes, differences between the sexes are assumed to have some genetic, neural, or hormonal source. Researchers are not required to specify what particular mechanisms are the source of sex differences, and when the mechanisms are specified and proved to be incorrect, they may be replaced by yet another untested biological cause (Shields, 1975).

2. One cannot prove the null hypothesis. Empirical methodology is based on a logic that states that nothing can be proved—something can only be disproved; for example, the fact that only females have babies does not prove that this will always be the case (indeed, advances in reproductive technology suggest the contrary). One single case of male pregnancy would definitively disprove the initial hypothesis. Psychologists interested in sex differences usually use a conventional statistical technique in which they postulate that no difference between groups exists (the null hypothesis) and then attempt to refute this hypothesis. This technique, however, does not allow one to discriminate between no difference because of flaws in experimental methodology or controls and no difference because the sexes are similar to each other. Editorial prejudice against the null hypothesis means that studies that find a difference are more likely to be published than those that do not (Kupfersmid, 1988). Hence, when supposedly ex-

tant sex differences are not found, the researcher cannot publish this and instead shifts to another phenomenon.

3. Examination of sex differences obscures the examination of sex similarities. For example, although Maccoby and Jacklin (1974) mentioned only four dependable sex differences in their extensive review of many areas in which sex differences had been studied, it is these four differences that have been consistently cited in textbook accounts of their work. The fact that the sexes are more similar than they are different is not considered noteworthy either by psychology as a discipline or by society as a whole.

4. Questions about sex differences often imply a trait view of behavior that obscures situational influences on behavior. Trait views of behavior assume that people carry a stable set of characteristics around with them so that there is consistency in the way that a particular person behaves in different situations. It is probably true that traits can predict behavior (especially when situational constraints are ambiguous), but it is unlikely that maleness and femaleness are stable traits. On the contrary, recent work in feminist psychology suggests that what we think of as gender is a complex mixture of traits, roles, and behavioral preferences influenced by situational demands (Spence, Deaux & Helmreich, 1985).

5. Research on sex differences does not concern itself with behaviors in which the rate is virtually zero for one sex. Thus, we do not find studies of sex differences in rape. Paradoxically, studies of sex differences concentrate on those areas in which males and females are seen as least different.

These criticisms are mostly conceptual in nature. Others have stressed methodological problems associated with the examination of sex differences. For example, Maccoby and Jacklin (1974) introduced the issue in their classic book on the subject with the following example:

We invite the reader to imagine a situation in which all psychological researchers routinely divide their subjects into two groups at random and perform their data analyses separately for the halves of the sample. Whenever a difference in findings emerges between the two groups (and this would of course sometimes happen by chance even when no difference exists that would replicate with further samples), our imaginary researcher tests the difference for significance, and any significant differences are included in the published report of the study. If we are not told that the original subdivision had been made at random, we might misspend a great deal of time attempting to explain the differences. (3–4)

Their book attempted to determine whether assigning cases to groups by sex is any more meaningful for understanding behavior than assigning them at random. Their conclusion was that consistent differences between males and females could be found in only a few cases. We should keep in mind, however, that although the criteria for the selection of human categories are not explicit in psychology, they are certainly not random. "From the large number of subject or organismic variables by which humans could be grouped only a few such as sex or race are chosen" (Unger, 1979b, 1087).

Sex and race are favored ways of categorizing people because of implicit theories of biological causality discussed above. People vary in other ways such as height, hair color, or physical attractiveness. These variations, however, are largely ignored because psychologists lacked a model to explain how such variables could influence behavior. As we shall see below, such external characteristics are becoming more popular in psychology as theories about the nature of social stereotypes and self-fulfilling prophecies have developed.

Researchers have identified a large number of methodological problems in the study of sex differences. Some of these were discussed in chapter 2 above. Problems include confusion between sex-of-subject and sex-of-experimenter effects (Jacklin, 1981). This kind of confusion can be clarified only when both female and male experimenters conduct studies with male and female subjects (a procedure that is not always followed even today). People appear to react differently to authority figures depending on whether the sex of the authority figure is the same or different from their own. Thus, Eagly (1978) demonstrated that male experimenters were more likely than female experimenters to find that women conformed more than men. Geis, Boston, and Hoffman (1985) found that while female college students in mixed-sex groups performed equally well for male and female experimenters, those who had interacted with male experimenters were unable to recognize their achievements in subsequent evaluations.

Other critics have focused on artifactual issues. Wallston and Grady (1985) noted, for example, that college students are the participants in most studies. Since young adulthood appears to be the age when differences between the sexes are maximized, choosing this group to study sex differences may inadvertently overrepresent these differences. Wallston and Grady also noted that the relationship between the topics studied and the sex of the sample chosen for study obscures the question of what sex differences might exist. Males, for example, are more likely to be chosen for research on aggression, whereas females are more likely to be chosen for research on affiliation. Thus, conclusions about, for example, sex differences in aggression may be based on a great deal of information about men and only a small amount about women.

Other researchers have demonstrated empirically that many sex differences can be attributed to sex-differentiated social contexts or differential social roles, not to qualities inherent in women and men. Deaux (1984), for example, has reviewed a considerable body of evidence showing that interactions with others can make sex more or less salient to the actor, depending on the expectations of the person with whom she or he is interacting. Eagly (1983) has reviewed evidence showing that men and women demonstrate traits usually associated with the same or other sex depending on the social role (for example, employer or employee) they are asked to fulfill at the time. These studies indicate that sex is not a particularly stable or global predictor of behavior and can predict behavior only because men and women are likely to be found in particular situations.

In spite of the general agreement of feminist psychologists that sex differences have a "now you see them, now you don't" quality (Unger, 1981), questions concerning differences continue to emerge. Since the number of possible differences is infinite, I propose to insert another set of questions for consideration: (1) Why do feminist psychologists remain so concerned with sex/gender differences when even the most impressive ones appear to account for little of the variability in human behavior? In order to answer this question we must look at how sex and gender are currently defined by psychology. (2) Can feminist psychologists exchange the study of sex/gender differences for forms of analyses that are compatible with feminist scholarship in other disciplines? In order to deal with this question we must examine how sex and gender are examined within the current positivist paradigm within psychology in contrast to the constructionist paradigms more popular with feminist scholars outside the discipline. (3) Is it possible to construct a theory and method of feminist psychology? In order to deal with this question we must examine the implicit structure of both psychological and feminist paradigms.

What Kind of Variables Are Sex and Gender?

THE NAME ISSUE

Feminist psychologists have not been consistent in the way they have defined sex and gender. The name issue has plagued the field of the psychology of women from its very inception (cf. Unger, 1979a). In general, feminist psychologists have attempted to narrow the definition of *sex* to include only those aspects of the individual that are clearly biologically based (i.e., characteristics associated with reproduction or sexuality) and to use the term *gender* to refer to those aspects of males and females for which biological causality has not been established (Unger, 1979b).

Unfortunately, even this kind of differentiation is problematic. First, it is difficult to establish causality for traits and behaviors that are the result of complex interactions between biological and social influences. For example, if early menarche is associated with poorer school achievement in girls, as has been found by some researchers (Brooks-Gunn & Petersen, 1983), we do not know if this effect is caused by hormonal events at puberty or if it is caused by the response of young men to young women's changing physical appearance.

Second, feminist psychology has inherited baggage from the field of psychology as a whole in terms of terminology about sex and gender. Earlier researchers did not make as many or the same distinctions as we do at present. Moreover, some of the terms such as *sex role* carry with them "an assortment of sociological and psychological data along with an explosive mixture of myth and untested assumptions" (Sherif, 1982, 392). The concept of sex role is curious because it couples a biological concept (sex) with a sociological term (role). "Thus, the concept suffers from double jeopardy from myths about sex smuggled in uncritically and from denotative confusions in the sociological concept of roles" (Sherif, 392).

Third, current research on the cognitive components of stereotypes suggests that sex serves as a stimulus that leads people to make assumptions about a wide variety of traits, roles, behaviors, and physical characteristics of individuals (Deaux & Lewis, 1984). These are often closely related to one another and no one domain appears to be any more important than any other as a base for generating sex-related hypotheses about people. Thus, sex as a categorization system appears to be integrally connected to assumptions about gender.

Possibly because of all the conceptual problems noted above, feminist psychologists have not agreed about what terminology to use. Some researchers use sex and gender as synonyms, some have replaced sex almost entirely by gender, and others continue to use terms such as sex role. For the purpose of this chapter, I use the word sex to refer to the categorization system of our society (reflected by psychology) that distinguishes two sexes—male and female. In this sense, most of the work I have discussed thus far has, indeed, been on sex differences.

THE DIFFERENCE BETWEEN SEX AND GENDER

Despite confusion in terminology, feminist psychologists have focused on gender more than on sex. This distinction is based on assumptions about causality that have not been made explicit until recently. Thus, studies on sex differences that derived from either a psychodynamic or individual-difference perspective assumed that the characteristic being studied was part of the individual's personality (Unger, 1989). Sex-related traits were seen as stable and coherent—as part of the essential nature of the person. These assumptions derived from a positivist-objectivist worldview (Flax, 1987).

Many feminist psychologists, however, recognized that sex forms the basis of a social classification system—gender. They realized that the traits and behaviors attributed to females and males had a prescriptive as well as a descriptive function (Pleck, 1981). They began to look for the origin of male-female differences within the social system rather than within the person. Thus, the study of gender represented a paradigm shift within psychology (Unger, 1983). The shift from the behavior of the sexes to the way the sexes are perceived reflected a shift in focus from existing social reality to the way that people construct social reality.

In this chapter, therefore, I define gender as a scheme for the social categorization of individuals (Sherif, 1982). Gender refers to the cognitive and perceptual mechanisms by which biological differentiation is translated into social differentiation. Since gender is defined here as a process rather than as something people possess, the term *gender difference* might produce some conceptual confusion. It is certainly not a synonym for sex difference because it derives from an entirely different view of social reality. In fact, it can be argued that the term should be retired from use because it reflects our society's construction of the sexes as different (Hare-Mustin & Marecek, 1988). At this time I use it sparingly to refer to beliefs about the way males and females differ in our society. Used in this sense, the term gender differences is very similar in meaning to the term gender stereotypes.

SEX AS A BIOLOGICAL CATEGORY

Psychologists have treated sex differences as found—not made. Epistemological assumptions embedded in psychology as it is currently practiced make it difficult to deal with gender as a process rather than as a phenomenon (Unger, 1989; in press). First, a primary definition of the field calls for the formulation of general laws from specific behaviors. In order to create such generalizations for highly variable human beings, one must find categories into which to fit them. Although no adequate theoretical justification for what determines a relevant or irrelevant psychological category has ever been formulated, biological sex has long been an unquestioned psychological variable (Rosenberg, 1982; Shields, 1975).

The use of biological sex as a major psychological category is problematic because of the extent to which it is confounded with differential social experiences, expectations, and so forth. These issues have been a major focus for feminist psychology since its very inception. What might be less clear is that the dichotomy of male-female based on biological sex is itself problematic. One can argue that there are more than two sexes in terms of the many biological criteria of sex, such as sex chromosome composition, hormones, and genital structure (cf. Unger, 1979a). Little attention is paid to this diversity in psychological studies. Sex—like race, but unlike many other psychological variables—is constructed as a dualism rather than as a continuum.

Recent studies on the cognitive structure of gender stereotypes illuminate the way that implicit assumptions influence our conceptions of sex. For example, when people were asked to describe the characteristics of male and female homosexuals, their descriptions were more similar to heterosexual individuals of the other sex than they were to heterosexual individuals of the same biological sex as the homosexual target person (Kite & Deaux, 1987). These results support an implicit inversion model of homosexuality based on people's bipolar beliefs about females and males. People appear to organize sex along a single dimension. They are willing to alter their beliefs about a person's traits, behaviors, and physical appearance rather than to accept a single component (sexual preference) that is divergent with their view of appropriate gender.

Interestingly, both the medical and mental health professions have had similar conceptual difficulty dealing with individuals for whom various designators of sex are not consistent with each other. It is only recently that psychology and psychiatry have acknowledged that homosexuality is not a priori evidence of psychological disturbance. And the medical establishment has been willing to undertake extensive surgical conversion of the bodies of transsexuals rather than to help them to come to terms with the idea that the psyche of one sex can coexist with the body of the other (Raymond, 1979).

SEX AS A TRAIT

It has been difficult for feminist psychologists to conceive categorization systems that ignore biological distinctions. Bem's (1974) concept of psychological androgyny (although flawed) represented a first attempt to distinguish between biological sex and a psychological component of sex-related identity for predicting the behavior of women and men. Instead of defining masculinity and femininity as opposite to each other, as had been done in the past, Bem devised a measure that defined them as independent of each other. Thus, biological males and females were able to evaluate themselves in terms of the extent to which they perceived themselves to possess the stereotypic traits of each sex. This procedure resulted in four categories based on various combinations of high and low amounts of male- and female-typed traits. Under some conditions, psychological profile (that is, sex-role self-concept) predicted behavior better than biological sex. People of both sexes with similar sex-role self-concepts were more like each other than they were like people of the same sex who differed in their self-conceptions.

Unfortunately, Bem's measure did not eliminate sex as a social reality. The traits she used remain those stereotypically associated with females and males. It is probably a measure of the strength of the socially prescriptive function associated with sex in our society that androgyny has come to be seen as a combination of the traits of the two sexes rather than as a transcendence of gender categorization itself.

Psychology as a field has been largely dependent on trait views about reality. Psychologists tend to conceptualize differences of any kind as intrinsic to individuals rather than as a result of interactions between them. Thus, feminist psychologists are caught in a dilemma peculiar to the discipline as a whole. For psychology, females and males differ because of what is within them. Feminist psychologists must deal with the evidential framework of trait theories involving sex differences if they hope to influence the rest of the field. Within this epistemological framework, the only feminist alternatives available are to construct trait theories that are either value-neutral or gynocentric. Both practices continue to reify the concept of difference.

Reframing questions about difference in terms of the more dynamic and interactive concept of gender would be more compatible with social constructionism and feminist scholarship in other fields. Gender in this sense could be defined as a verb. Reframing the questions, however, is done at the risk of deviation from a basic premise of psychology—the idea that gender is a thing or an entity—a noun.

Feminist criticism of the conceptualization of sex and gender by psychology is beginning to move from methodological to epistemological issues. Critics have moved from suggestions as to how methodology could be improved to discover what is really due to sex or gender to alternative, more conceptual questions. These questions involve the nature of psychology as a discipline as well as the nature of our implicit assumptions as both feminists and psychologists. How does the structure of psychology as a discipline force us to deal with sex and gender as though they were entities rather than processes? What hidden epistemological assumptions lead even feminist psychologists to the implicit acknowledgment of biological causality? And can feminist selections of categories for analysis themselves be value-free?

What Are Male-Female Differences?

Feminist researchers have begun to examine the way in which language and research methodology are used to create the concept of sex difference. Even using the operational tools of classical experimental psycholoy, for example, there has been no agreement as to what are the proper criteria for a sex difference. Some of the unresolved questions are: How large a difference constitutes a meaningful distinction as opposed to a statistical one? How many individuals within one sexual category must differ from those in the other for a sex difference to be said to exist? Must sex differences persist across situations? To what extent must they be generalizable across age or culture? What would happen to our data base on sex and gender if we asked these questions?

Attempts have been made using the relatively new technique of meta-analysis to determine the existence and size of various sex differences. Meta-analysis is a statistical technique that enables a researcher to summarize many different and independent studies testing the same hypothesis—in this case the hypothesis of a reliable sex difference in some cognitive or social behavior. Advocates of this method (cf. Eagly, 1987; Hyde & Linn, 1986) argue that the quantitative integration used eliminates problems associated with bias in the selection of studies as well as bias in the evaluative criteria used to determine when a difference exits. Thus, meta-analysis offers an opportunity to evaluate the magnitude of differences in particular behavior with a methodology that is more even-handed than a narrative review (in which the researcher collects as many published studies as she can find and summarizes their results). Meta-analysis also uses more information than simply counting the number of times a difference is found.

There is, however, much current controversy in the literature about the meaning of effect sizes and the degree of variability in behavior that can be accounted for by them. For sex-difference analyses, effect size is a statistic that represents the magnitude of a sex difference in each study. It is expressed in standard deviation units. Effect size is the difference between the means of the male and female groups divided by the within-group standard deviation. As an extensive discussion of this statistic is beyond the scope of this chapter, it may be thought of as a ratio of male-female differences to male-male and female-female differences. If males and females differ from each other more than they do from other members of their own sex, the effect size of the study will be large. (Eagly, 1987 contains a fuller discussion of the technical aspects of meta-analysis.)

Eagly (1987) argues that feminist researchers have systematically underestimated the number of sex differences found because of their ideological predispositions. She bases her argument on an examination of effect sizes obtained through meta-analyses of sex differences in a number of areas of social behavior (in particular, those of influenceability, helping, and aggression). She argues that the amount of variability in these behaviors that is explained by sex is comparable to that found by social psychologists for variables that they can manipulate, for example, the kind of task required, the size of the group being studied, the sex of the experimenter, and so forth. Sex, then, has as much influence on social behavior as many other psychological variables. She also argues that the difference between the percentage of people of each sex who engage in sex-typed behaviors is large enough to be noticeable and helps form the basis for people's perception of the extent of sex differences.

In contrast, Hyde and Linn (1986) focus on the degree of variability that can be predicted on the basis of effect sizes. They suggest that most sex-related differences are quite small in terms of the total variability in a given behavior. Even for behaviors that consistently appear to show sex differences (such as aggression), sex appears to account for only 5 percent of the variability between people.

The debate surrounding meta-analysis is valuable because it illustrates some of the factors that influence how psychologists decide that a given difference makes a difference. Decisions are greatly influenced by what one uses as a comparison group. Sex, for example, is comparable in importance to other psychological variables. It is not, however, particularly important in comparison to all the independent variables that influence any particular human behavior. This controversy demonstrates that the use of quantitative methodology (as specified by the positivist-empiricist model of science) does not eliminate the necessity for qualitative judgment.

Meta-analysis also assumes that sex-related traits and behaviors have an existence independent of the social contexts in which they are found. Feminist psychologists have just begun to evolve theories that treat social context as a psychological variable. Many, perhaps most, sex-related differences emerge in some environments but not in others. The presence of other people seems to have an important effect. I discuss this in more detail below. The way many sex-related behaviors change according to the social environment, however, casts further doubt on whether such differences exist within the person.

It is clear that critiques of methodology alone do not go far enough. Moreover, questions such as those asked in meta-analyses become meaningless in a frame of reference that views gender as a verb rather than as a noun. Traits and behaviors linked to sex are constructed by on-going interactions between people. Sex-related characteristics within the person influence his or her interactions, but the major determinants of sex-related behaviors are the expectations, social roles, and demands conferred on the individual by his or her social sex. This is what feminist sociologists (cf. West & Zimmerman, 1987) mean by "doing gender."

Gender is created by social processes. When social demands are strong enough, people will behave in sex-characteristic ways whether or not they possess the sex-typed traits supposedly directing their behavior. Thus, social demands can function as self-fulfilling prophecies. Sometimes, however, the social demands imposed by gender are so strong that they continue to constrain behavior even when people are alone. We label ourselves by sex and prefer that our behavior be consistent with that label. According to this view, on-going social interactions are key for constructing gendered behavior; traits that have been socialized within the person over a long period of time play a secondary role.

Gender and Thought

The concept of doing gender is compatible with the current cognitive paradigm within psychology. This paradigm has moved away from behavior as the major unit of analysis and has focused on so-called inside the head phenomena; for example, perceptions, thoughts, and memories. Within the study of sex and gender, the focus has moved away from a description of behaviors as structural-functional entities (traits) and toward an analysis of the social contexts that elicit sex differences in behaviors. In this section of the chapter, I discuss current findings on some of these contexts.

THE SEX COMPOSITION OF GROUPS

Studies during the past decade suggest that gender-related behaviors are more likely to emerge in public than in private. An early study in this area demonstrated that men and women differed in the way they distributed rewards to others, depending on whether they made their decisions in a group or by themselves (Kidder, Belletirie & Cohn, 1977). In groups, women were more likely to allocate rewards equally, whereas men were more likely to concur with a norm of equity—reward distribution based on the amount produced by each person in the group. In private, however, both sexes deviated from the sex-characteristic pattern of allocation and became more like the other: Men appeared to be more willing to distribute rewards equally, whereas women were more likely to use equity as a basis for rewards.

In a later study of the effect of public scrutiny on sex-related differences in behavior, Eagly, Wood, and Fishbaugh (1981) found that expected sex differences in conformity (women conformed more than men) were found only when men and women were exposed to social-influence attempts in groups. In private, women were no more likely to be influenced than were men. Interestingly, the women's degree of conformity was the same in public and private contexts. Men's behavior, however, was altered by the context—they were as conforming as women in private, but were less conforming than women in public. The researchers suggested that conformity should be relabeled. Instead of women's greater conformity, we should speak of men's greater tendency to deviate from others' opinions. Cultural norms of male individuality and autonomy may impel men to make public displays of their ability to differ from the group.

The apparent fluidity of behavior across situational contexts makes it difficult to describe behavioral traits as built-in or even as the result of long-term differences in the socialization of the sexes. How could such hypothetical traits be so easily modified by social demands? What is important about public contexts is that they encourage or even necessitate conformity to social norms about gender.

The sex composition of the social context appears to be a major factor in the salience of gender; for example, when people were asked, Who are you? whether and how they used sex to describe themselves depended on whether they believed the category made them distinctive within a group. McGuire, McGuire, and Winton (1979) found that people were most likely to use sex as a primary way of identifying themselves when their sex was a statistical minority within their family or classroom. Thus, a girl whose siblings were all brothers was more likely to use sex in her self-description than a girl with both brothers and sisters. Hair color and ethnicity were other characteristics that were used in this manner.

People may use their sex to make themselves distinctive under some conditions, but they appear to minimize their differences from the majority when their minority status might make them vulnerable. In transient rather than customary groups, people of the minority sex use more traits associated with the majority sex in their self-descriptions than do individuals in more sex-balanced groups (Higgins & King, 1981; Ruble & Higgins, 1976). Minority status may be celebrated only when people feel secure about their place within a group.

SEX AS A SELF-FULFILLING PROPHECY

These studies demonstrate that sex is never invisible in a social situation. People use information about the sex composition of the various groups of which they are a part even when sex is not an explicit component in their social interactions. Still other studies show how sex-related behaviors can be created by the expectations of those with whom individuals interact. Skrypnek and Snyder (1982), for example, placed students in situations in which they interacted with unseen partners whom they believed to be either male or female. Male students assigned tasks to their partners differently depending on whether they believed the partner was male or female. Moreover, beliefs about a partner's sex produced sex-stereotypic behavior in the partner, for example, individuals whose partners believed they were female were more subordinate and accommodating than those whose partners believed they were male.

There have been a number of important studies demonstrating the self-fulfilling nature of sex-related behaviors. These studies show that people will alter their styles of self-presentation when interacting with those who have an important evaluative function in their lives. Zanna and Pack (1975), for example, demonstrated that female students altered their self-descriptions in the direction of femininity when they believed that an attractive potential dating partner held traditional views about women. No such change occurred when the potential partner was thought to be either nontraditional or unattractive. In a naturalistic experiment involving a job application, Zanna and his associates (Von-Baeyer, Sherk & Zanna, 1981) found that women wore more make-up and jewelry for a job interview with a man portrayed as having traditional attitudes about women than with a potential employer portrayed as having egalitarian views. These studies suggest that important aspects of gender are socially created and that so-called sex differences emerge in response to expectations of others in a particular situational context.

INDIVIDUAL DIFFERENCES IN SEX-RELATED PERCEPTIONS

People appear to be unaware of the extent to which gender influences their self-perceptions and their lives. Spence and Sawin

(1985), for example, have found that although people appeared to find questions about their own masculinity or femininity self-evident or meaningless, they had little difficulty in making judgments about the masculinity or femininity of others. Moreover, identical questions involving sex discrimination were answered differently for oneself than for others (Crosby, 1982; Unger & Sussman, 1986). Women appeared to be well aware of unequal treatment when it applied to others but tended to overlook its applicability to themselves.

People may also differ in the extent to which they use gender to construct reality. Sandra Bem has revised her ideas about her androgyny scale so that she now describes it as a measure of the extent to which people draw on gender stereotypes in descriptions of themselves and others, not as a measure of built-in sex-related traits. She defines people who show a stereotypical pattern of trait ratings (high in masculine and low in feminine traits for males; high in feminine and low in masculine traits for females) as sex-typed or gender schematic.

Bem and others have carried out many studies demonstrating that people who are gender schematic (those who spontaneously organize information about themselves in a traditional sex-typed way) differ in a number of ways from those who are not. They processed sex-consistent information about the self more easily than inconsistent information. They were more likely to remember information in terms of categories organized by gender (e.g., when they recalled lists of words that included some with gender associations, they were more likely to clump groups of words by gender than aschematic individuals). They were also more likely to use sex-typed behavioral styles in their interactions with others (LaFrance & Carmen, 1980; Lippa, 1978) and to make use of information correlated with gender in our society. Gender-schematic people, for example, paid more attention to physical attractiveness (highly correlated with perceptions about gender in our society). They were also more positive toward physically attractive people, especially those of the other sex (Andersen & Bem, 1981; Lippa, 1983).

The extent to which males and females differed was influenced by their self-perceptions. Gender-schematic or sex-typed men and women were more different in their helping behaviors than were men and women who were aschematic (Senneker & Hendrick, 1983). Bem (1985) suggests that many of the supposed sex differences found in many studies are actually due to the presence of sex-typed males and females, who predominate in any sample of subjects studied as well as in society as a whole.

Bem's research illustrates how our concepts about the relationship of individual differences to the study of gender have progressed. But it also illustrates the limitations of this approach. Her concept of androgyny untied certain aspects of gender roles (so-called masculinity and femininity) from biological sex. Bem's newer concept of gender schema places the origin of sex differentiation in a cognitive rather than a personological framework. Both conceptualizations, however, remain descriptive. Further, they remain based on an epistemology that assumes a relatively fixed, consistent individual. Little attention has been paid to the role of the situation in eliciting sex-differentiated beliefs about oneself or others.

Feminist researchers working within a social-cognitive framework have demonstrated that sex and gender as informational systems serve as a major means to evaluate others, to communicate expectations about each other, and to guide one's own behavior even when the social context does not appear to be gender-relevant. But we know that sex and gender labels are applied differently depending on the situational context (public vs. private), group composition (cf. Dion, 1985), sex of the stimulus person, and whether the self or another is the referent. Rather than regard these inconsistencies as an excuse to assume that gender is too unstable to be usefully analyzed, we can explore the workings of gender as a form of social contradiction and the implications of such contradiction for gender as a mechanism of social control (cf. Henley, 1977; Unger, 1983; Unger, 1988).

Social Constructionism as an Alternative to Social Cognition

The acknowledgment of contradiction as a fundamental part of social reality is consistent with theoretical frameworks that make use of some form of social constructionism (cf. Gergen, 1985) or postmodernist philosophy (cf. Flax, 1987). Social constructionism, for example, stresses the way in which social categories or processes are produced by the use of language or the selective use of evidence—for example, what questions are asked as well as how the answers are interpreted. Social constructionism can be seen as an alternative to positivist epistemology, which asserts that realities are discovered rather than created.

A social-constructionist perspective within psychology differs from purely traditional approaches in several ways. Such a perspective argues, for example, that psychological phenomena must be understood in terms of their historical or situational specificity—that they have no abstract existence apart from the context in which they occur or are studied. Thus, it is meaningless to compile the results of many studies of what is presumed to be the same phenomenon, as in meta-analysis, in order to arrive at general statements about its existence. Social constructionists would also argue that several different definitions of important categories such as sex and gender can operate simultaneously in a particular situation. Differing perspectives can be present among the various participants in a social interaction or even within a single individual, depending on which aspects of these categories are salient at a particular time. Thus, researchers can expect to obtain different definitions depending on how they frame their questions or shape the context in which the questions are asked. These are not methodological flaws but an integral part of the processes by which sex and gender are continually redefined.

A social-constructionist approach to psychology also leaves room for feminist political analysis to influence theory and practice directly rather than by way of the selection of a content area or problem to be studied. Since phenomena can be interpreted only in terms of current circumstances, current social arrangements must enter into psychological analysis. This kind of formulation prevents us from believing that factors that influence choices and limit lives are "all in our heads" and helps to explain consistencies in female realities without resorting to biological explanations. Virtually all women exist within a social hierarchy in which "male is greater than female."

From a social-constructionist standpoint, sex and gender are complex descriptive and prescriptive processes. They are both internalized and communicated to others. Neither sex or gender, however, is integrally whole or internally consistent. The problem for feminist psychologists, therefore, is to determine under what conditions a particular definition is salient. When, for example, is a particular definition of gender a mechanism of social control that exerts influences on most individuals of a particular sex? What enables individuals to resist definitions of gender in particular circumstances? And why are only some social definitions of sex and gender incorporated into our views of ourselves?

These problems are at the heart of the relationship between the person and society. Psychologists have wrestled with these issues for many years without resolution. There is no reason why feminist psychologists should attempt to resolve them de novo. It might be helpful to examine conceptualizations developed by feminists in other disciplines. In a recent article, for example, Gerson and Peiss (1985) suggest that we study the societal function of gender in three areas: boundary maintenance, social negotiation, and domination and consciousness. These are mechanisms that regulate cross-sex interactions. Consideration of them might be helpful in delineating the different levels at which sex and gender can be defined.

On a societal level, for example, boundaries between the sexes are maintained by the sex-segregation of occupations. On a smaller scale, the sexes are separated by implicit rules about interpersonal gestures and styles. Women are expected to use a less assertive style than men and violators can be viewed as sexually aggressive rather than interpersonally assertive (Unger, 1979a). Perceptions and misperceptions about the meaning of nonverbal behaviors for women and men appear to function in a way that maintains power asymmetries between the sexes. It is surely no accident that one of the first and fundamental feminist insights in psychology involved interpersonal touching and the confounding of sex and status in our society (Henley, 1973).

On an interpersonal level, processes involving social negotiation appear to be very important in producing and maintaining sex differences. Men have control over a great share of resources and opportunities so that women's ability to negotiate for societal equity is restricted by their limited access to such resources. Negotiation for interpersonal equity is also restricted by social norms and punishments for gender deviance. Perceived penalties for deviance might account for the sex-related differences in public and private behavior discussed above. There seems to be increasing evidence that women will behave as competitively as men when rewards for doing so are available to them (cf. Keller & Moglin, 1987).

Societal arrangements that make women more responsible for everyday life can influence their consciousness of it. Women's supposedly more concrete and relational perceptions might be their response to the persistent need to negotiate for a place in a male-dominated world. Different worldviews also serve to separate the sexes. Feminist psychologists can contribute to our understanding of such processes by elucidating the psychological mechanisms by which gender exerts control at these various levels of analysis. Power is clearly an important part of the social context at each of these levels.

Gender and Contradiction

Contradiction can be a particularly interesting area to explore in terms of a social-constructionist theory of consciousness. For example, an individual may be well aware that gender deviance will not be allowed even if only a few instances of gender-inappropriate behavior are punished. Widespread media attention to such cases as that of Mary Cunningham, an attractive Harvard M.B.A. who rose "too rapidly" in the Bendix Corporation, can make it clear to other women that high aspirations and physical attractiveness do not go together. For working-class women, magazines such as *True Story* include many (35 percent) stories about rape and attempted assault—which usually occur when the woman has been in the wrong place, has chosen not to accept advice, or has acted too independently (Cantor, 1987).

Feminist psychologists have begun to develop a typology of situations and circumstances in which gender-appropriateness is likely to be noticed and judged (cf. O'Leary, Unger & Wallston, 1985). This involves distinguishing contexts in which any female is seen to be out of place and when it is "only" her behavior that will be devalued rather than her presence (Unger, 1988). For example, women are accepted in work environments in which women predominate but are more likely to report being sexually harassed in nontraditional jobs with highly unequal sex ratios (Gutek & Cohen, 1987). We still need, however, to identify the form and circumstances in which negative judgments about members of one's social category are incorporated into one's personal identity.

I have argued elsewhere (Unger, 1988) that contradictions in terms of how and when gender is socially salient make it difficult to develop an accurate self-knowledge. A kind of tyranny of structurelessness makes it difficult for a woman to determine whether a negative response is a consequence of her social category or of her personal behavior. Since negative responses often occur in situations where women are isolated, they might find it impossible to validate their perceptions with others like themselves. Our very language has many more terms for differences in personal characteristics than for differences in situational constraints. Thus, women might be more likely to assume personal responsibility for their behavior and its consequences and, therefore, blame themselves rather than seek social explanations and social change.

Contradictions within definitions of femininity create double binds for women that do not seem to exist for men in our society. Socially acceptable feminine behavior has negative social consequences because it conflicts with perceptions of instrumentality and adulthood (Broverman, Vogel, Broverman, Clarkson & Rosenkrantz, 1972). As noted above, however, feminine behaviors are demanded via the expectations of others, and so-called self-fulfilling prophecies confirm these expectations.

Imagine a woman viewing her own behavior from the perspective of an outside observer (although few or no other members of her social category are likely to be present under circumstances in which social mechanisms that create sex differences are most potent). She might see herself as confirming feminine stereotypes of dependency, oversensitivity to others, or emotional lability. Without observing other women behaving in a similar way under similar conditions, she might well explain her behavior as the result of her personal deficiency—the explanation fostered by cultural norms. It is important to keep in mind that her perception of her own behavior may be correct, but her explanations of it are wrong. It might be preferable for her self-esteem, however, to accept complicity in behaviors that can have harmful consequences rather than to see herself as controlled by others.

Experimental social psychology provides some useful techniques for analyzing gender as an interactional phenomenon. It provides some ways to evaluate the claims of theories that posit the existence of gender differences as opposed to those contending that gender differences are created. It is difficult to argue, for example, that so-called gender differences in conformity are the product of long-term socialization if they emerge or disappear as a function of whether people's behavior is observed by others. Comparison of behavior in private and public provides a way to bring social norms into the laboratory. It also provides a way to study the effect of social context while holding social roles constant.

It is important that we do not regard perceptions and cognitions about sex and gender as individualistic phenomena. People cannot alter their inadequate or inappropriate views of the world at will. It is also important that we not neglect the role of the social framework in creating these perceptions. Each of these caveats is important in light of psychologists' propensity for conceptualizing human problems on a personal level.

The Construction of Social Reality

One way in which feminist psychologists can challenge psychology's tendency to accept difference as a given is to demonstrate the enormous extent to which both our professional and cultural categories are constructed. Examples can be found at every level of analysis. Historians of science have noted that throughout the nineteenth and most of the twentieth century, estrogen was called "the female hormone" despite the fact that the richest source of this hormone was the urine of stallions (Hall, 1977). Anthropologists tell us that not all societies have two genders derived from two sexes. In some kinship systems, age is the major differentiator, and words referring to gender have meaning only with reference to specific adult reproductive roles (Gailey, 1987). In other societies, it is possible for a female or a male to take on the role and the gender of the other sex. What differences in social organization emerge when gender is viewed as modifiable?

It is not necessary to go to other societies to find different cognitions about gender. Transsexuals, for example, appear to see their sex, but not their gender, as modifiable. Social psychologists have, however, been reluctant to study cognitive frameworks in a so-called deviant population. This unwillingness is partly a function of the fact that social psychology derives from a nomothetic tradition—it seeks to extract general rules for behavior rather than to examine the individuality of particular persons. It is probably also a function of our cultural definition of sex and gender as a highly correlated system, as unmodifiable, and as internally consistent. Other ways of defining sex/gender have been made to disappear (Flax, 1987).

Even among so-called normal males and females, perceptions involving gender vary with race, social class, and even geographic region. Black women, for example, generally expect that they will hold paying jobs as adults (Turner & McCaffrey, 1974) and are less likely than white women to see marriage and motherhood as incompatible with work outside the home (Murray & Mednick, 1977). It is important that we do not obscure the differences between particular groups of women in our examination of women's differences from men.

Dichotomies between male and female or masculine and feminine are constructed by selective research—by bias in our research methodology as well as in the populations chosen for research. Methods that allow subjects to respond freely indicate a much greater range of meanings for gender. In an extensive anthropological study of Southern college students, for example, Holland and Skinner (1987) found that both sexes had a complex, implicit categorization system for gender types that classified both the evaluator and those he or she evaluated. Females appeared to classify males in terms of how likely they were to use their position or attractiveness to females for selfish purposes;

how ineffectual or unlikable they were; and how unusual their sexual appetites were. Males classified females in terms of their prestige as valued sexual possessions or companions; their tendency to be overdemanding or engulfing; and their sex appeal. Obviously, such typing has utility for the social system in which college students interact, but it has little resemblance to beliefs about males and females tapped by conventional psychological methodology.

When two sexes are not clearly demarcated, people seem to invent them. In a clever experiment designed to manipulate assumptions about gender rather than simply to measure them, John and Sussman (1984–85) asked subjects to take the role of a participant during several stages of a narrative involving a social interaction between two persons whose sex was unspecified. Sometimes "brown buttons" made assertive or initiative-taking statements and sometimes "gray buttons" did. The researchers found that subjects made assumptions about the heterosexual nature of the transaction even at the expense of role consistency or the integrity of the narrative. They also inferred role reciprocity so that when one participant was assumed to be male, the other automatically became female.

The Applicability of Social Constructionism to Psychology

It can be difficult for psychologists to accept the social construction of such an apparently basic phenomenon as gender. This is partly because of a continuing positivist epistemology within the field as well as a confusion between sex and gender. Variables that have physical reality such as neurons, hormones, and physiological sex appear as more *real* than purely psychological processes. It has been suggested that psychology suffers from "physics envy."

It is probably no accident that Naomi Weisstein, author of a pioneering constructionist critique of psychology's treatment of women in 1968, is also well known for her research on the neural bases of optical illusions. Using the figure-ground illusion—an ambiguous situation in which two perceptions alternate although the physical stimulus remains the same—she has shown that discrimination of an additional faint stimulus imposed on the illusion is better within the figure than the ground irrespective of where that figure may be at the time (Wong & Weisstein, 1982). Weisstein (1970) has also demonstrated that adaptation to an entire grid of lines (so that the intensity of stimulus required to perceive all parts of the grid is greater) occurs even when part of that grid has been blocked by a cube. She has suggested that this phenomenon represents a kind of symbolic activity in neurons— a neuronal awareness that something is in back of something else.

Although these studies would appear to have nothing to do with gender, they demonstrate that some forms of subjective construction take place at a very basic physiological level. Such findings have no place in a theory that states that physiological mechanisms reflect reality. They demonstrate, however, that constructionist explanations can be useful at all levels of psychology and that constructionist processes are not any less real than other psychological phenomena.

An additional barrier to understanding the constructed nature of gender in our society is the continuing tendency of psychologists to dichotomize both sex and gender. As noted above, this is probably a reflection of the kinds of questions psychologists ask and the methods they use to analyze the answers. But dichotomies are also metaphors for the way we structure reality. The terms *male* and *female* carry with them beliefs about good and evil, rational and irrational, and so forth. Some of these metaphors can be extracted by psychological methodology that permits subjects to choose their own categories when they are making evaluations about the sexes. Such techniques applied to gender reveal a "dark side" to stereotypes that reflect implicit assumptions about dominance and sexuality not unlike those voiced by Southern college students described above (Ashmore, 1981). Beliefs about male hardness and female softness probably exert as much social control over the sexes as do societal prescriptions about appropriate gender-role behavior. Indeed, these negative beliefs can exert even more powerful social control because they are subject to neither conscious scrutiny nor public debate.

Sex Differences and Feminist Psychology

MEASUREMENT ISSUES IN PSYCHOLOGY

If it is so easy to find an alternative framework in which to explore gender as a social process, why does the issue of sex differences remain particularly problematic for feminist psychologists? Although part of the problem is psychology's epistemology, part is also the nature of the relationship between psychology and the rest of society. Our society appears to have charged psychology with the measurement of the normative characteristics of human beings. The enormous impact of psychological definitions and measures of intelligence on such social institutions as schools and the army has led psychologists to apply similar operational assumptions to such personality traits as sexual identity (Pleck, 1981).

Neither psychology nor society as a whole, however, distinguished between description and prescription in these measures. Thus, psychology became the academic discipline that judged the normality and adequacy of individual human beings. Although the dominant paradigm within American psychology—behaviorism—was not explicitly part of the individual difference-intelligence testing movement, its ahistorical and unreflective nature (cf. Unger, 1989) helped to mask the issue of what factors determined the variables on which individuals were differentiated. Why, for example, were race, sex, and ethnicity preferred variables, whereas social class and physical structure were ignored?

Although only a relatively small part of psychology is still directly concerned with the measurement of individual differences, most psychological practitioners are concerned with helping the individual adapt himself or herself to the needs and norms of society. Clients in counseling and psychotherapy are keenly aware of differences between themselves and others. Difference, in this sense, is equated with deficiency. And members of some groups continue to be seen as more socially deficient than others. It is difficult for psychologists engaged in the practice of helping others to question the assumptions that define their professional role. Even feminist psychologists have not always avoided the "woman-as-problem" paradigm; see, for instance, the extensive literature on fear of success and the need for assertiveness training for women (Crawford & Marecek, 1989).

The response of some feminist scholars—both psychologists and those in other disciplines—has been to argue for the subject's different but equal voice (cf. Gilligan, 1982). In the absence of explanatory mechanisms for differences between dominant and oppressed groups, however, such theories remain a more sophisticated version of individual-difference or trait paradigms. Definitions of superior or inferior characteristics continue to surface (in sex, as in race, there appear to be no separate but equal categories), and the power to define remains with those in the dominant categories. Few female scholars have the power to name (Stimpson, 1979).

I believe with Gilligan that women's (and others') voices have often gone unheard in professional dialogues. The issue that is so divisive for feminist scholars is whether any human group can be said to speak in a different voice. Are there reifiable aspects of group membership (biological or social) that are related to consistent and universal variations in social behavior? This issue poses particular problems for feminist psychologists. Can psychology as a discipline exist if we can make no general rules?

THE IDIOGRAPHIC AND NOMOTHETIC TRADITIONS

Is social constructionism the answer? It has had a great impact in fields such as history, literary criticism, and anthropology (cf. Stacey & Thorne, 1986), because the principle of telling the individual's story is an accepted aspect of these disciplines. Description and narrative are familiar tools. Description and narrative are characteristic of what is known to psychologists as the idiographic approach (cf. Allport, 1968). This approach focuses on the special characteristics of the individual—the ways that she or he is unique rather than similar to other human beings. Within psychology, however, the idiographic approach has been largely limited to the study of personality.

As those of us within psychology are aware, there have always been two psychologies—one characterized by the idiographic approach and one characterized by the so-called nomothetic approach, that is, by the attempt to extract general laws from the study and analysis of a large number of randomly selected individuals (cf. Brewer & Collins, 1981). These two psychologies differ from each other in values and world outlook as well as in methodology (Kimble, 1984). There has been little agreement between them on whom to study and how to do so. In the one area of psychology where both approaches have been used—the study of personality—theories have frequently floundered when situational variability is taken into account.

Telling an individual's story is a familiar form of the idiographic approach. It is this form that is best known to feminists outside of psychology. There are problems with the approach, however, for such feminists as myself who have been trained in a more nomothetic tradition. Whose story should be told? This problem has been ignored by psychologists who tell stories about people who exemplify a point the narrator wishes to make. Such story telling leaves the reader at the mercy of the selection criteria (often unspecified and even unrecognized) of the narrator.

It is not clear whether the idiographic approach can be used effectively in areas other than the study of personality. How do we describe the unique qualities in each encounter between individuals? The number of stories we would have to tell is infinite. And again, we might be accused of bias based on the selection criteria of the narrator.

The idiographic approach might be inconsistent with a theoretical position, such as my own, that argues that social context constrains behavior. Thus, many people in the same social category will respond the same way in certain contexts. This approach argues that some generalities in human beings must be acknowledged although one must study individuals as well. Some aspects of the social context can be examined using the tools of social constructionism devised for the study of individuals; for example, social contexts can be defined differently by participants depending on their needs and on the social roles that are salient in that context. But different people might define contexts similarly if they have similar needs and social roles. Feminist psychologists must develop methods that give participants in our research the opportunity to define their situation freely and the tools to determine the similarities or differences in their definitions.

Unfortunately, nomothetic methods have been equated by some feminists with constraint of the individual's ability to select freely among alternatives. This is sometimes known as *context stripping*. Some methods discussed below permit researchers to infer results from open-ended responses, but these methods require a great deal of statistical and quantitative manipulation. As noted in my discussion of meta-analysis above, the use of complex quantitative tools does not free us from the need to make qualitative judgments. Moreover, since quantitative methods often require a great deal of expertise, it is difficult for the nonexpert to judge whether or not covert values have influenced the decisions made.

Feminist suspicion of nomothetic methods is matched by experimental psychology's suspicion of qualitative techniques. One issue involves the relative status of research methods in experimental psychology. Most research psychologists prefer quantitative and experimental methods, so-called hard science, over qualitative methods, or so-called soft techniques (Wallston, 1981). Feminist theorists have argued for methods with subjective, experiential, and qualitative elements (Wilkinson, 1986). Feminist psychologists, however, have continued to publish studies using rather traditional experimental methods (Lykes & Stewart, 1986). There can be insurmountable problems in attempting to translate constructionist methods into tools of social psychology. But feminist psychologists who wish to communicate with both feminists outside psychology and nonfeminists within it will have to adopt a strategy that involves an integration of quantitative and qualitative methods in conjunction with a critical examination of the relationship between the two.

FEMINISM AND THE ISSUE OF COMPARISONS

In several points I have discussed the concept of the comparison group as a major factor in our decisions about whether a particular sex difference exits. The ability to offer meaningful comparisons is an important contribution that feminist psychologists can make to feminists in other disciplines. Since, however, comparisons require that some differences must be ignored, it is easy to misunderstand the role of comparison in psychology and to charge that researchers interested in quantification have oversimplified and overgeneralized findings about males and females. Nevertheless, comparison can be the fundamental tool by which feminist scholarship can escape a kind of radical relativism—in which we can make no generalizations at all.

Feminist psychologists will have to transcend the current dichotomy between an approach that focuses on the specific qualities of each woman (and thus permits only description) and an approach that focuses on generalities (and thus permits global statements about sex differences). To do so, we must generate studies that simultaneously compare groups in a number of different ways. Instead of simply comparing women to men, we need to compare black women to white women, heterosexual women to lesbians, and working-class women to affluent women. But we also need to compare groups of men and women that we believe to be similar in various ways. Comparisons of this sort in terms of occupational roles suggest that men and women are not particularly different (Powell, 1987). What is important here is that we specify ahead of time why each comparison is useful.

Who we compare to whom is a fundamental question in the psychology of sex and gender. In an early paper in this area, Parlee (1981) pointed out that conclusions about whether males and females differed in health were affected by whether the group chosen for comparison with affluent, well-educated, successful males was their sisters (who were presumably biologically similar but in different social roles) or unrelated females in comparable occupational roles. Datan (1986), in a reappraisal of her important work on midlife transition of women from various subcultures in Israel, noted the failure to investigate the husbands of her respondents because funding agents at the time were primarily concerned with the consequences of what they defined as a strictly biological event—menopause. Both of these studies illustrate implicit assumptions about the importance of biological determinants—assumptions that influenced the comparison groups selected and thus influenced their results.

Experimental psychology is based on comparisons. Reliability, for example, refers to a comparison of the same research population to itself to determine whether a measure shows consistent effects over time. Validity has many meanings but generally refers to comparisons between psychological instruments believed to measure similar aspects of behavior. Replicability—the cornerstone of empirical investigation—involves comparisons of independent studies to see if the same results are produced. These concepts are limited by their assumption that people remain constant over time and place and do not react to being examined by different researchers. Nevertheless, they give us a framework on which generalizations can be examined. For example, the failure of projective measures of achievement to predict the achievement-related behavior of women in the same way as that of men (a failure of validity) led to the development of the concept of fear of success and an extensive literature on gender and achievement. Similarly, inconsistency between various measures of androgyny (a failure of reliability) has led to questions about the meaning of the concept. Failures in replicability have also led to questions about the existence of sex-related differences in moral development.

The useful comparisons for feminist psychologists include:

1. A comparison of the same behaviors in different social contexts. Eagly (1987) has suggested that the laboratory environment of psychological studies can produce a greater amount of gender differentiation because it strips participants of other social roles. It could be, however, that the role of subject overrides gender awareness and can reduce some sex-related differences (Unger, 1981). The laboratory as a social context deserves special attention (cf. Morawski, below).

2. A comparison of behavior carried out under public scrutiny as compared to behavior believed to be private. Studies summarized earlier suggest that the presence of others causes an invasion of social norms that enhances gender differentiation.

3. A comparison of sex-ratios in groups, as well as comparisons between transient and permanent groups. Dion's (1985) preliminary analysis of group processes suggests that these two variables together produce either gender assimila-

tion or distinctiveness. People appear to emphasize distinctiveness when their place within a group is secure (such as within the family or classroom), whereas they minimize gender differences when they are in a minority in transient groups. We need to pay special attention to the position of token as the most extreme example of being a minority in any kind of group.

4. A comparison of what people say about themselves in terms of sex and gender and what they say about others. Spence and Helmreich (1978) report that there is no relationship between how people rate their own instrumental and affective qualities and the extent to which they generate sex stereotypes about these qualities for others. People appear to perceive themselves as less sex-typed than they perceive others. If so, estimates of sex differences in some characteristics associated with gender will vary depending on whether the referent is the self or others.

All of these comparisons involve investigating gender as a phenomenon rather than gender as a difference. The universality of gender differences can, however, also be tested by comparisons between people of different races, social classes, and ethnic backgrounds. Investigation of the constructions of gender in different cultures and subcultures is, of course, fundamental as is the development of research techniques that permit us to go beyond dichotomization. One such technique is the Q sort, in which people are permitted to rank a variety of statements in terms of their importance or relevance. Kitzinger (1986) used this methodology to evaluate the meaning of lesbianism for a group of self-defined lesbians. She found that lesbianism had a range of meanings from a source of self-fulfillment and inner peace through political self-definition to a self-definition based on belief in personal inadequacy or failure. This methodology provides a rich picture of important differences within groups and could certainly be used to understand differences between them. But as

Kitzinger warns, it is, like any research strategy, at the mercy of the researcher's judgment, since she has selected the statements or categories to be sorted.

Any method using comparison must ignore many important differences among individuals. It is the reliance on some form of categorization that has led feminists outside of psychology to accuse psychologists, including feminist psychologists, of context stripping and ignoring the unique features of individuals. But comparisons carefully done, with the criteria for group selection made explicit, can focus the debate in terms of what is truly unique to women and to men, or, more correctly, careful comparisons can focus the debate on the question, What aspects of gender produce the particular qualities being measured at this time? Unfortunately, because methods involving multiple comparisons often involve what is seen by those outside the discipline, as arcane statistical manipulation, they will be less easily integrated with feminist scholarship as a whole than are the narrative techniques discussed below.

FEMINIST PSYCHOLOGY AND THE INDIVIDUAL'S STORY

A promising and quite different avenue of research involves the growing concern of feminist psychologists with various forms of narrative and personal stories. Such studies place the individual within her time and place. Although some of these analyses are akin to literary ones, substituting experience for text, psychological concepts are used to illuminate the material. Thus far, these integrations appear to have been most successful in analyzing developmental issues for women. Helson (1983–84), for example, has used Jungian theory to elucidate critical points in the lifespan of individual women. She points to correspondences between changes in the work of creative women and age-related changes in their life circumstances. Stewart (1987) has used the concept of historical cohort to explain personality dynamics in successive generations of women. She suggests that unique historic events that were important at critical periods in women's development influence what is important to them at a later stage. Thus, it is meaningless to compare women of the same age across generations unless we take into account the historical events that occurred at critical points in their lives.

One means of integrating narrative measures with more conventional psychological measures involves comparing structured and nonstructured questions. In nonstructured cases the respondents provide the narrative to be analyzed. Sanders and her colleagues (Sanders, Steil & Weinglass, 1984–85), for example, gave traditionally religious women vignettes in which married career women made decisions that had a negative impact on their careers. They found that although their respondents apparently favored choices that "preserved the family" when measured by objective scales, these women also showed considerable anger about such choices when their subjective responses were evaluated. In contrast, Crawford (1988) found that sex differences in humor production were the same whether she used structured or less-structured methods. These varied findings suggest that we do not yet know enough about psychological methodology to prescribe or proscribe a particular kind of research.

Feminist psychologists are also attempting to make their involvement with their research more explicit and reflexive. This process has been termed *conscious subjectivity* (Wilkinson, 1986). Dialogue by the researcher both with the participants in the research and with its hypothetical audience illuminates the way that the researcher's assumptions have constructed the particular reality being examined. Thus, Fine (1983–84) shows us how her beliefs about effective coping following rape are a product of her white middle-class position in society. In her account of an extended conversation in a rape crisis center, she reveals as much or more about herself than she discloses about the black woman who has just been raped. Similarly, Marshall (1986) shows us how she became more feminist and more accepting of qualitative research as she progressed through her research on the experiences of women managers. Last, Lykes (1989) illustrates some of the problems produced when the researcher and participants have different constructions of reality. She analyzed the response of Guatemalan Indian women to an informed consent form regularly used by psychologists to insure ethical treatment of their subjects. Use of a written form, however, violated the oral tradition of the Indian women and resulted in a loss of trust. Each of these narratives portrays the intrusion of the researcher into her research and thus explodes the myth of objective science.

The use of narrative opens up as many problems for feminist psychologists as it resolves; for example, what criteria do we use to determine whose story should be told? What yardsticks do we use to measure the reliability of personal reality when we know that people constantly reconstruct themselves as their personal circumstances and awareness change? If everyone has his or her own version of reality, what criteria do we use to determine the most useful definition of reality? Of course, the key question here is: Useful to whom?

Nomothetic vs. Idiographic Methodology: In Praise of Diversity

The issue of how much individual reality we must sacrifice to attain consensual reality has long been a divisive one for psychologists. It is probably absurd to believe that feminist psychologists can resolve the issue, but we might be able to transcend it. To do so, we need to understand what the issue is. The issue is fundamentally one of variability and the extent to which individuals vary within themselves. I have argued in this chapter that various aspects of sex and gender cannot be defined as either global or invariant for any individual. It is only by using definitions that reduce the contradiction and inconsistency within individuals that we are able to maximize differences between them. In addition, it is only by using definitions that ignore differences within groups that we are able to maximize differences between them. Thus, if we concentrate on individuals—on how people within a given sexual or racial category differ from each other—we will be less able to look at such categories in terms of global differences.

These problems are fundamentally unresolvable. Any attempt to gain more fine-grained analysis in one area will result in the loss of information in another. Better methodological and conceptual tools will not resolve the paradox. If psychology is to envy physics, perhaps it should be for its embrace of uncertainty. We may need to construct feminist psychological paradigms that are more akin to quantum physics—that is, to abandon the belief that a particular construct can be located in a specific time or place. We may also need to accept the idea that not only are multiple answers to a question produced in various theoretical frameworks, but other answers will evolve as circumstances change and new paradigmatic frameworks become important. It is difficult for those of us trained in a positivist empiricist framework to accept the position that no one perspective is ever true.

Feminist scholarship has to shrug off an even older tradition if it is to accept contradiction as a foundation for a different view of reality. A basic tenet of Aristotelian logic is that something cannot be both true and not true. Paradox is not permitted within this system. Yet psychologists are well aware that paradoxes in the form of optical illusions, for example, do occur. The value of paradoxes is that they lead to questions about the nature of a system that can produce such perceptual traps.

I have always been struck by the large number of feminist articles and books that include in their titles references to mirrors, prisms, lenses, looking glasses, and so forth. At some level we have all been aware that reality is reflected in a variety of ways. The sexes will be as different or as similar as we want them to be. Knowledge exits only as the product of the questions asked. Multiple perspectives will produce multiple answers.

One of our basic tasks is to make sure that the answers we get and use are not based on the values and self-interest of any single component of society—even ourselves. It is not meaningful to ask: What are the *true* differences? They are all a result of smoke and mirrors.

REFERENCES

Allport, G. W. (1968). *The person in psychology: Selected essays*. Boston: Beacon Press.

Andersen, S. M. & Bem, S. L. (1981). Sex typing and androgyny in dyadic interaction: Individual differences in responsiveness to physical attractiveness. *Journal of Personality and Social Psychology, 41*, 74–86.

Ashmore, R. D. (1981). Sex stereotypes and implicit personality theory. In D. L. Hamilton (Ed.), *Cognitive processes in stereotyping and intergroup behavior*. Hillsdale, NJ: Erlbaum.

Bem, S. L. (1974). The measurement of psychological androgyny. *Journal of Consulting and Clinical Psychology, 42*, 155–62.

Bem, S. L. (1985). Androgyny and gender schema theory: A conceptual and empirical investigation. In T. B. Sonderegger, (Ed.), *Nebraska Symposium on Motivation, 1984: Psychology and gender* (179–226). Lincoln: University of Nebraska Press.

Brewer, M. B. & Collins, B. E. (Eds.) (1981). *Scientific inquiry and the social sciences: A volume in honor of Donald T. Campbell*. San Francisco: Jossey-Bass.

Brooks-Gunn, J. & Petersen, A. C. (Eds.). (1983). Girls at puberty. New York: Plenum Press.

Broverman, I. K., Vogel, S. R., Broverman, D. M., Clarkson, F. E. & Rosenkrantz, P. S. (1972). Sex-role stereotypes: A current appraisal. *Journal of Social Issues, 28*, 59–78.

Cantor, M. G. (1987). Popular culture and the portrayal of women: Content and control. In B. B. Hess & M. M. Ferree (Eds.), *Analyzing gender* (190–214). Newbury Park, CA: Sage.

Crawford, M. (1988). Humor in conversational context: Beyond biases in the study of gender and humor. In R. K. Unger (Ed.), *Representations: Social Constructions of Gender* (155–66). Amityville, NY: Baywood.

Crawford, M. (1989). Agreeing to differ: feminist epistemologies and women's ways of knowing. In M. Crawford & M. Gentry (Eds.), *Gender and thought* (128–45). New York: Springer-Verlag.

Crawford, M. & Marecek, J. (1989). Psychology reconstructs the female: 1968–1988. *Psychology of Women Quarterly, 13*, 147–65.

Crosby, F. (1982). *Relative deprivation and working women*. New York: Oxford University Press.

Datan, N. (1986). Corpses, lepers, and menstruating women: Tradition, transition, and the sociology of knowledge. *Sex Roles, 14*, 693–703.

Deaux, K. (1984). From individual differences to social categories: Analysis of a decade's research on gender. *American Psychologist, 39*, 105–16.

Deaux, K. & Lewis, L. L. (1984). Structure of gender stereotypes: Interrelationships among components and gender label. *Journal of Personality and Social Psychology, 46*, 991–1004.

Dion, K. L. (1985). Sex, gender, and groups: Selected issues. In V. E. O'Leary, R. K. Unger & B. S. Wallston (Eds.), *Women, gender, and social psychology* (293–347). Hillsdale, NJ: Erlbaum.

Dion, K. L. (1986). Responses to perceived discrimination and relative deprivation. In J. M. Olson, C. P. Herman & M. P. Zanna (Eds.), *Relative deprivation and social comparison: The Ontario Symposium* (Vol. 4). Hillsdale, NJ: Erlbaum.

Eagly, A. H. (1978). Sex differences in influenceability. *Psychological Bulletin, 85*, 86–116.

Eagly, A. H. (1983). Gender and social influence: A social psychological analysis. *American Psychologist, 38*, 971–81.

Eagly, A. H. (1987). *Sex differences in social behavior: A social-role interpretation*. Hillsdale, NJ: Erlbaum.

Eagly, A. H., Wood, W. & Fishbaugh, L. (1981). Sex differences in conformity: Surveillance by the group as a determinant of male nonconformity. *Journal of Personality and Social Psychology, 40*, 384–94.

Fine, M. (1983–84). Coping with rape: Critical perspectives on consciousness. *Imagination, Cognition, and Personality, 3*, 249–67.

Flax, J. (1987). Postmodernism and gender relations in feminist theory. *Signs, 12*, 621–43.

Gailey, C. W. (1987). Evolutionary perspectives on gender hierarchy. In B. B. Hess & M. M. Ferree (Eds.), *Analyzing gender: A Handbook of social science research* (32–67). Newbury Park, CA: Sage.

Geis, F. L., Boston, M. B. & Hoffman, N. (1985). Sex of authority role models and achievement by men and women: Leadership, performance, and recognition. *Journal of Personality and Social Psychology, 49*, 636–53.

Gergen, K. J. (1985). The social constructionist movement in modern psychology. *American Psychologist, 40*, 266–75.

Gerson, J. M. & Peiss, K. (1985). Boundaries, negotiation, consciousness: Reconceptualizing gender relation. *Social Problems, 32,* 317–31.

Gilligan, C. (1982). *In a different voice.* Cambridge, MA: Harvard University Press.

Gutek, B. A. & Cohen, A. G. (1987). Sex ratios, sex role spillover, and sex at work: A comparison of men's and women's experience. *Human Relations, 40,* 97–115.

Hall, D. L. (1977). *Social implications of the scientific study of sex.* Paper presented at the symposium "The Scholar and the Feminist IV," Barnard College, 23 April 1977.

Hare-Mustin, R. T. & Marecek, J. (1988). The meaning of difference: Gender theory, postmodernism, and psychology. *American Psychologist, 43,* 455–64.

Helson, R. (1983–84). E. Nesbit's forty-first year: Her life, times, and symbolization of personality growth. *Imagination, Cognition, and Personality, 3,* 53–68.

Henley, N. M. (1973). Status and sex: Some touching observations. *Journal of the Psychonomic Society, 2,* 91–93.

Henley, N. M. (1977). *Body politics: Power, sex, and nonverbal communication.* Englewood Cliffs, NJ: Prentice-Hall.

Higgins, E. T. & King, G. (1981). Accessibility of social constructs: Information-processing consequences of individual and contextual variability. In N. Cantor & J. F. Kihlstrom (Eds.), *Personality, cognition, and social interaction.* Hillsdale, NJ: Erlbaum Associates.

Holland, D. & Skinner, D. (1987). Prestige and intimacy: The cultural models behind Americans' talk about gender types. In D. Holland & N. Quinn (Eds.), *Cultural models in language and thought.* New York: Cambridge University Press.

Hyde, J. S. & Linn, M. C. (Eds.). (1986). *The psychology of gender: Advances through meta-analysis.* Baltimore: Johns Hopkins University Press.

Jacklin, C. N. (1981). Methodological issues in the study of sex-related differences. *Developmental Review, 1,* 266–73.

John, B. A. & Sussman, L. E. (1984–85). Initiative taking as a determinant of role-reciprocal organization. *Imagination, Cognition, and Personality, 4,* 277–91.

Keller, E. F., & Moglen, H. (1987). Competition: A problem for academic women. In V. Minor & H. E. Longino (Eds.), *Competition: A feminist taboo?* (21–37). New York: Feminist Press.

Kidder, L. M., Belletirie, G. & Cohn, E. S. (1977). Secret ambitions and public performance: The effect of anonymity on reward allocations made by men and women. *Journal of Experimental Social Psychology*, *13*, 70–80.

Kimble, G. A. (1984). Psychology's two cultures. *American Psychologist*, *39*, 833–39.

Kite, M. E. & Deaux, K. (1987). Gender belief systems: Homosexuality and the implicit inversion theory. *Psychology of Women Quarterly, 11*, 83–96.

Kitzinger, C. (1986). Introducing and developing Q as a feminist methodology: A study of accounts of lesbianism. In S. Wilkinson (Ed.), *Feminist social psychology: Developing theory and practice* (151–72). Stony Stratford, England: Keynes.

Kupfersmid, J. (1988). Improving what is published: A model in search of an editor. *American Psychologist, 43*, 635–42.

LaFrance, M. & Carmen, B. (1980). The nonverbal display of psychological androgyny. *Journal of Personality and Social Psychology, 38*, 36–49.

Lippa, R. (1978). The naive perception of masculinity-femininity on the basis of expressive cues. *Journal of Research on Personality, 12*, 1–14.

Lippa, R. (1983). Sex typing and the perception of body outlines. *Journal of Personality, 51*, 667–82.

Lykes, M. B. (1989). Dialogues with Guatemalan Indian women: Critical perspectives on constructing collaborative research. In R. K. Unger (Ed.), *Representations: Social constructions of gender* (167–85). Amityville, NY: Baywood.

Lykes, M. B. & Stewart, A. J. (1986). Evaluating the feminist challenge to research in personality and social psychology: 1963–1983. *Psychology of Women Quarterly, 10*, 393–412.

Maccoby, E. E. & Jacklin, C. N. (1974). *The psychology of sex differences.* Palo Alto: Stanford University Press.

Marshall, J. (1986). Exploring the experiences of women managers: Towards rigour in qualitative methods. In S. Wilkinson (Ed.), *Feminist social psychology: Developing theory and practice* (193–209). Stony Stratford, England: Keynes.

McGuire, W. J., McGuire, C. V. & Winton, W. (1979). Effects of household sex composition on the salience of one's gender in the spontaneous self-concept. *Journal of Experimental Social Psychology, 15*, 77–90.

Murray, S. R. & Mednick, M. T. S. (1977). Black women's achievement orientation: Motivational and cognitive factors. *Psychology of Women Quarterly, 1*, 247–59.

O'Leary, V. E., Unger, R. K. & Wallston, B. S. (Eds.). (1985). *Women, gender, and social psychology.* Hillsdale, NJ: Erlbaum.

Parlee, M. B. (1981). Appropriate control groups in feminist research. *Psychology of Women Quarterly, 5*, 637–44.

Pleck, J. (1981). *The myth of masculinity.* Cambridge, MA: MIT Press.

Powell, G. N. (1987). The effects of sex and gender on recruitment. *Academy of Management Review, 12*, 731–43.

Raymond, J. G. (1979). *The transsexual empire: The making of the she-male.* Boston: Beacon Press.

Rosenberg, R. (1982). *Beyond separate spheres: Intellectual roots of modern feminism.* New Haven: Yale University Press.

Ruble, D. N. & Higgins, E. T. (1976). Effects of group sex-composition on self-presentation and sex-typing. *Journal of Social Issues, 32*, 125–32.

Sanders, A., Steil, J. & Weinglass, J. (1984–85). Taking the traditional route: Some covert costs of decisions for the married career woman. *Imagination, Cognition, and Personality, 4*, 327–36.

Senneker, P. & Hendrick, C. (1983). Androgyny and helping behavior. *Journal of Personality and Social Psychology, 45*, 916–25.

Sherif, C. W. (1982). Needed concepts in the study of gender identity. *Psychology of Women Quarterly, 6*, 375–98.

Shields, S. A. (1975). Functionalism, Darwinism, and the psychology of women: A study in social myth. *American Psychologist, 30*, 739–54.

Skrypnek, B. J. & Snyder, M. (1982). On the self-perpetuating nature of stereotypes about women and men. *Journal of Experimental Social Psychology, 18*, 277–91.

Spence, J. T., Deaux, K. & Helmreich, R. L. (1985). Sex roles in contemporary American society. In G. Lindzey & E. Aronson (Eds.), *The handbook of social psychology* (3rd ed.) (149–78). New York: Random House.

Spence, J. T. & Helmreich, R. L. (1978). *Masculinity and femininity.* Austin: University of Texas Press.

Spence, J. T. & Sawin, L. L. (1985). Images of masculinity and femininity: A reconceptualization. In V. E. O'Leary, R. K. Unger & B. S. Wallston (Eds.), *Women, gender, and social psychology* (35–66). Hillsdale, NJ: Erlbaum.

Stacey, J. & Thorne, B. (1985). The missing feminist revolution in sociology. *Social Problems, 32*, 301–16.

Stewart, A. J. (1987). *Some consequences of the things our mothers did and didn't teach us: Social and individual change in women's lives.* Invited address at the Meeting of the Eastern Psychological Association, Crystal City, VA.

Stimpson, C. R. (1979). The power to name: Some reflections on the Avant-Garde. In J. A. Sherman & E. T. Beck (Eds.), *The prism of sex:*

Essays in the sociology of knowledge (55–77). Madison: University of Wisconsin Press.

Turner, B. F. & McCaffrey, J. H. (1974). Socialization and career orientation among black and white college women. *Journal of Vocational Behavior, 55,* 307–19.

Unger, R. K. (1979a). *Female and male: Psychological perspectives.* New York: Harper & Row.

Unger, R. K. (1979b). Toward a redefinition of sex and gender. *American Psychologist, 34,* 1085–94.

Unger, R. K. (1981). Sex as a social reality: Field and laboratory research. *Psychology of Women Quarterly, 5,* 645–53.

Unger, R. K. (1983). Through the looking glass: No Wonderland yet! (The reciprocal relationship between methodology and models of reality). *Psychology of Women Quarterly, 8,* 9–32.

Unger, R. K. (1988). Psychological, feminist, and personal epistemology: Transcending contradiction. In M. M. Gergen (Ed.), *Feminist thought and the structure of knowledge* (124–41). New York: New York University Press.

Unger, R. K. (1989). Sex, gender, and epistemology. In M. Crawford & M. Gentry (Eds.), *Gender and thought* (17–35). New York: Springer-Verlag.

Unger, R. K. (In press). The selection of method and content in psychology: The contribution of feminism. In J. Hartman & E. Messer-Davidow (Eds.), *Critical issues in feminist inquiry.* Washington, DC: Modern Language Association.

Unger, R. K. & Sussman, L. E. (1986). "I and thou": Another barrier to societal change? *Sex Roles, 14,* 629–36.

Von Baeyer, C. L., Sherk, D. L. & Zanna, M. P. (1981). Impression management in the job interview: When the female applicant meets the male "chauvinist" interviewer. *Personality and Social Psychology Bulletin, 7,* 45–51.

Wallston, B. S. (1981). What are the questions in psychology of women?: A feminist approach to research. *Psychology of Women Quarterly, 5,* 597–617.

Wallston, B. S. & Grady, K. E. (1985). Integrating the feminist critique and the crisis in social psychology: Another look at research methods. In V. E. O'Leary, R. K. Unger & B. S. Wallston (Eds.), *Women, gender, and social psychology* (7–33). Hillsdale, NJ: Erlbaum.

Weisstein, N. (1968). *Kinder, Kuche, Kirche as scientific law: Psychology constructs the female.* Boston: New England Free Press.

Weisstein, N. (1970). Neural symbolic activity: A psychophysical measure. *Science, 168,* 1489–91.

West, C. & Zimmerman, D. H. (1987). Doing gender. *Gender & Society, 1,* 125–51.

Wilkinson, S. (Ed.). (1986). *Feminist social psychology: Developing theory and practice.* Stony Stratford, England: Keynes.

Wong, E. & Weisstein, N. (1982). A new perceptual context-superiority effect: Line segments are more visible against a figure than against a ground. *Science, 218,* 587–89.

Zanna, M. P. & Pack, S. J. (1975). On the self-fulfilling nature of apparent sex differences in behavior. *Journal of Experimental Social Psychology, 11,* 583–91.

5

Toward the Unimagined:

Feminism and Epistemology in Psychology

JILL G. MORAWSKI

In spite of a sustained interest in questions of gender and a proliferation of empirical studies, there have been no fundamental changes in our conceptualization of gender. Psychological knowledge about gender continues to depend on core axioms of socialization, role acquisition, stereotypes, femininity, and masculinity. During the past fifteen years feminist perspectives have brought some methodological correctives (Lykes & Stewart, 1986); other than these, there have been no notable reformulations of our models of gendered behavior. In the face of the tremendous personal and intellectual challenges of feminism, the psychological perspective on and analysis of gender have remained unchanged, as have the foundational metatheory and epistemology. Does this stability mean that the scientific tenets underlying gender research are without the kinds of androcentric bias found in other areas of science and social science? Can a feminist psychology of gender thus proceed on the preexisting epistemological edifice?

These questions frame one objective of this chapter: to assess the extent to which conventional psychological research on gender has been influenced by advances in feminist theory. Because modern feminism has challenged the philosophic foundations of thought, particular attention is given here to epistemological issues. The other objective, apparent in the chapter's title, is to contemplate how the psychology of gender might be reimagined in light of feminist inquiry in other disciplines that has yet to be extended to conventional psychology.

Both of these objectives assume the need to change the superstructure of the psychology of gender. Feminist research throughout academe has indicated the central importance of the very work practices implied when we say that we are "doing psychology" (or any disciplinary work) or that we are "developing psychological theory"—that is, to speak about feminism and epistemology is to do more than to assess values and intellectual assumptions. To imagine feminist knowledge seeking therefore means reconsidering the social relations of our work: a reconstruction of the game, along with its rules and activities, especially as they implicitly align our actions as researchers with existing valences of social power. Given this turn from epistemology to practice, an aim underlying this chapter is to consider how the social relations constituting psychological work might change.

Studies of gender now constitute a massive research program in psychology; even state-of-the-art meta-analyses (see Eagly, 1987) cannot yield a complete sense of the production. Nevertheless, most of research coheres, primarily because it adheres to a certain theoretical orientation that, in turn, follows shared epistemological and methodological premises. An example of this research program and its premises is found in studies of androgyny, an area of investigation that both incorporates the premises of conventional research and yet has been fueled significantly by feminist thinking.

As an entrance into these multiple objectives, androgyny research is reviewed to exemplify how feminism has merged with the mainstream rudiments of psychological work. The subsequent section explores several of the less acknowledged aspects of research practice and assesses the constraints these practices impose on the generation of new theory. The final section considers the nature of scientific work practices and invites the reader to imagine other possibilities.

The Impasse of Androgyny

Sandra Harding (1986b) has suggested that there are three fundamental ways in which feminists have addressed the question of science: the creation of feminist empiricism, standpoint (women-centered) feminism, and feminist postmodernism. Within psychology the predominant mode of redress has been feminist empiricism. Like the other modes, feminist empiricism begins with recognition that sexism exists as a social problem and, in science in particular, as a social bias in research. Given that the methodological norms of science function to eliminate personal or social bias, feminist empiricism is unique in suggesting that sexism is correctable by stricter adherence to these norms. There is a general sense that women researchers are more likely to recognize sexist bias and, therefore, to become committed to the proper functioning of the scientific method. Although not discussed by Harding, concomitant with this recognition is a related belief that sound empirical research will also reveal sexist biases in psychological processes and social practices. A further aspect of this feminist research is the related belief that if the observer is cleansed of biased perceptions, then a more accurate account of the observable, empirical world would be made and, ultimately, a more just social policy would be implemented. As with the scientific method, the structural norms of the social order are taken to be unproblematic once they are rid of such imposed biases as sexism.

Androgyny research illustrates how feminist empiricism typically has been implemented in psychology. The development of the concept of androgyny began with efforts to remove the biases of sexist methods and constructs. In the early 1970s researchers conducted systematic critiques of the gender traits, masculinity and femininity. They questioned whether these gender attributes really are bipolar and mutually exclusive, whether assigned biological sex is somehow the determinant of appropriate gender traits, and whether identity between biological sex and gender characteristics is necessary for psychological adjustment. Encompassing both methodological and theoretical dimensions, these criticisms indicated that research on masculinity and femininity, along with the measurement scales employed in that research, was value laden. The values embedded in this research were those that assumed gender *difference*, some essential qualities of what it meant to be male or female. The research privileged the idea of two distinct psychological genders that were (and ought to be) consistent with one's biological sex and stable across the life span. Consistent with these values was the implicit assumption that deviation from the norms of gender-role identity was not normal.

The concept of androgyny was posited as a corrective to these value biases. Androgyny, a combination of feminine and masculine attributes, eliminated assumptions of gender dualism that had served as markers for some underlying yet real gender differences. The concept does not assume any appropriate linkages between biological sex and psychological gender, nor does it entail claims about sexual orientation. This idea of gender further supplies a model for social policy: While the original concept of gender attributes contains norms of male and female behavior, the androgyny model offers a vision of flexible, successful human agents operating in a complex, nongender-structured social world. Regarding these social norms, it is important to note that although investigators generally perceived that these conceptual developments eliminate certain value biases, at least one researcher (Bem, 1974) explicitly proposed androgyny as a concept consistent with feminist values. Undoubtedly many other researchers have adopted the concept for its emancipatory qualities: Androgyny afforded more emancipatory notions of appropriate behavior and mental well-being.

Judging by the wide usage of masculinity-femininity scales revised to incorporate androgyny, the androgyny concept appealed to psychologists seeking to remedy bias in gender studies. This emerging research avenue generated serious problems, however, and the literature on androgyny soon indicated that the new measurement devices produced numerous theoretical and psychometric complications. First, there was little understanding of precisely how femininity and masculinity combined to form this newly recognized type of social agency: Is androgyny the result of additive processes, that is, so much femininity plus so much masculinity; is it the interaction of some particular aspects of the two gender attributes; or is it the result of reaching some threshold of these attributes? Related to these conceptual issues was the fact that the androgyny model continues to acknowledge and even depend on the conventional concepts of femininity and masculinity. Thus, in spite of its emancipatory promise, the model retains the classic dualism and, hence, the assumption of some real gender difference. The revised psychometric tests thus objectify this dualism and claim to assay some real inner psychological entities.

Another problematic feature of androgyny emerged from both empirical studies and critical analyses (reviewed in Morawski, 1987). What was introduced as the possibility of a flexible, enabling, even gender-free personhood revealed an uncomfortable resemblance to masculine qualities: Just as quantitative analysis suggested that masculinity scores were a fair predictor of androgynous behavior, so qualitative analyses illuminated individualist, male-centered ideals underlying the concept. Androgyny at once appeared to maintain gender dualism and perpetuate a set of cultural ideals favoring a particular type of social agency, that of a cognitively flexible, independent, and self-contained individual. Seen in terms of the feminist empiricist goals of removing sexist bias, androgyny research is particularly revealing: Correcting biases resulted in a model that apparently is weighted toward masculine attributes and is consistent with social roles of an independent and instrumental social agent. These asymmetrical standards seem to address the dilemma of the professional woman, for they enable an agent to assume instrumental tasks while retaining feminine, expressive qualities (Morawski, 1985). Viewed from this perspective, the case of androgyny research reflects some ironic features of feminist empiricism. First, the removal of biased ideas was realized through replacement by other values, and, second, the complicated process of eliminating male biases resulted in a model that apparently privileges masculinity. This is not the first time in recent history that feminists' use of androgynous imagery backfired (Gubar, 1981; Smith-Rosenberg, 1985).

In psychology, the feminist empiricist program principally has entailed the removal of unscientific bias, but we must recognize what scientific practices are left unexamined. Above all, feminist empiricism does not challenge fundamental assumptions about the subjects of investigations or about the observers. It does not question the rudiments of the scientific method in psychology, for instance, those of observation, analysis, prediction, and generalization. Owing to the peculiar history of psychology, subjects can be seen as naive, unknowing, and often even incapable of accurate reporting. In contrast, the observers came to be taken as knowing, informed, and capable of accurate self-monitoring (Morawski, 1986, 1988a). The history of masculinity and femininity research illustrates how these assumptions are translated into the procedures of scientific work: Methodological controls were developed to blind subjects to the intent of the study; they rest on a basic doubt about the subjects' ability to knowingly assess their gender attributes and its consequences for behavior. These same controls simultaneously enabled researchers (notably through quantification and complex psychometrics) to have special access to the subjects' inner experiences of gender (Morawski, 1985). Other assumptions about subjects and the knowledge-generating process also remain unquestioned. For instance, androgyny research, like so much other research on gender, adopts the belief in the transhistorical stability of psychological processes and the relative unimportance of the specific context in which behavior and its psychological interpretation transpire. Some empiricist researchers have questioned specific aspects of these research axioms, for instance, Eagly (1978) demonstrated the historical nature of gender differences in conformity and Deaux and Major (1987) have suggested ways in which situational features are determinant of gender-appropriate behavior. A closer look at the history and practices associated with empiricism, however, suggests that such corrective measures will not resolve the problem of gender.

Where Is the Gender Problem?

Androgyny research has met with success and popularity; these must be recognized as feminist gains. In fact, it is worth momentarily bracketing the structural problems of the feminist empiricist program to acknowledge its gains. The progress has been of two sorts. Above all, work from a feminist empiricist stance represents some of the most astute critiques of contemporary experimental psychology. The critical analyses of research on hormones and behavior (Parlee, 1973; 1982), conformity (Eagly, 1978), field dependence (Haaken, 1988), and sex differences in the brain (Bleier, 1984; Fausto-Sterling, 1985, Mc-Clone, 1980), among other research areas, have provided thorough indictments regarding faulty theory, methods, and interpretation. These critical studies employ technical skill and sophisticated empiricist logic; their relative obscurity among psychologists outside the subcommunity of feminist psychology is regrettable but telling. The second area of accomplishment has been contributions to the understanding of women's lives. Examples of the many innovative projects include studies of individual development (Stewart, 1980), moral judgment (Gilligan, 1982), eating disorders (Striegel-Moore, Silberstein & Rodin 1986), and communication (Thorne & Henley, 1975; Lakoff, 1975). In spite of their contributions to conventional theorizing, these new inquiries seem to have limited currency and are known primarily within the domain of the psychology of women/gender. There seem to be boundaries on the achievements of feminist empiricist research.

Like other proposed correctives to conventional empirical research, the androgyny model has drawn attention to serious voids and misrepresentations in conventional theorizing. Such correctives constitute narratives of restoration for they challenge and remove detected bias and restore the natural story of scientific ethos and progress. Yet contained in this revisionist research, in the narratives of restoration, is evidence of the inherent failure of empiricism for feminism. It is understandable that androgyny research, like other similar programs, has come to an impasse. The various research impasses of these empiricist studies indicate that feminist thinking must confront other problems that are located at the core of scientific practice.

The problems requiring confrontation have a history with discernible patterns. Over the last two centuries women have turned to science because it was thought to offer a community in which they could participate (Rosenberg, 1982; Rossiter, 1982). Science promised a workplace and a form of knowledge seeking where personal attributes—race, sex, ethnicity—were irrelevant to one's participation. Modern knowledge, in Ruby Riemer's (1986) words, offered a "philosophical seduction" of the daughter. This seduction entailed the women's adoption of male rules that somehow contained "a promise of selfhood and inclusion in some philosophical community which, as women alone, they fully fail to achieve" (58). Riemer has argued for the necessity of knowing the full implications of this seduction: the adoption of and alliance to make ideals that are often alien to women's own experience. The history of women in psychology illustrates this seduction. The history also reveals some of the unanticipated consequences of women's entrance into the discipline. In order to avoid continuing the seductive trap and to organize alternative ways of working as scientists, we need to become familiar with the consequences of our status and relationship within empiricist communities.

Examination of some of the experiences of women in psychology provides vantage points for exploring how these experiences both epitomize and contribute to the limits of feminist thinking in psychology. Before highlighting these consequences, it should be noted that women (including feminists) who entered into the practice of psychology have tried to work largely within (or to rescue) the tenets of empiricism. From psychology's first generation of women advocates of women onward, few deviated notably from the core scientific beliefs in objective observation and the possibility of accurate, verifiable (or falsifiable) theories. The predominant experience of feminist psychologists, then, is marked by *adherence* to the conventions of a larger philosophical project. Those few feminists who did challenge this project or its rules of scientific practice received no audience within the discipline and most of their work went unnoticed and certainly unappreciated (Agronick, 1988; Trigg, 1987; Wittenstein, 1987).

Among the experiences of women entering psychology has been *social marginality.* Women of the early twentieth century who often were inspired by feminist visions, and who successfully acquired the skills and credentials of the new psychology, nevertheless were marginalized. Articulation of these crippling social relations was hindered by the avowed democratic ethos of science coupled with these workers' enthusiasm, especially during the formative period of female participation in science. Recent historical work recounts how the women's lives were marked by conflicts and exclusions. By tracing the lives of a number of these women, Scarborough and Furumoto (1987) have identified two basic issues; the conflict between personal attachments and career autonomy, and the denial of opportunity. Scarborough and Furumoto's study brings outstanding detail to the ways in which these women confronted professional barriers, from the case of Margaret Floy Washburn's reluctant recognition that meritocracy in science was a myth to the difficult and unsuccessful efforts of Ethel Puffer and Milicent Shinn to reconcile the demands of family and career. Women's exclusion was often overt as well as indirect; for example, Furumoto (1988) has traced the official exclusion of women from one prestigious society, Experimental Psychologists, between 1904 and 1929.

Historical studies of women in psychology and related professions indicate that women participants had to practice special strategies to compensate for marginality and possible exclusion. Rossiter (1982) has documented some of the common patterns of women's careers within the laboratory structure of academic science: While the early generation of women often ended up in areas designated as women's work, later generations found employment as associates to well-known researchers within large research endeavors or as researchers engaged in their spouses' projects. From their historical investigations, Glazer and Slater (1987) identified specific strategies that enabled women to acquire and retain professional positions. Women succeeded in attaining careers by undertaking innovative ventures that had no existing expertise, taking subservient posts or research activities, or choosing isolated, separate occupations, that is, working in women's colleges or in distinctly women's fields such as nursing. The result of these strategies of marginality, however, was double-edged; Glazer and Slater found that the researchers survived successfully, but they did so at the cost of limiting or excluding the generation of intellectual progeny to carry on the research ventures.

Women's marginal position in scientific professions has had other consequences. One of the most valued remedial measures, especially recently, has been the mentoring process whereby a senior, established woman scholar serves to advise a younger one in the sociopolitical nuances of career making as well as in her intellectual development. As noted above, in an organizational structure where women have often had limited access to the training of progeny, mentoring cannot always function as desired. Thus, for mentors and their younger colleagues, the process can be frustrating, although the frustrations can be quite different. Further, as a special form of role model, mentoring can foster the illusion of an employment system that is unconditionally open to women if they receive appropriate preparations. Fisher (1988) has provided a lucid exploration of these and related consequences and contradictions in women's search for role models.

Another, quite different consequence of women's marginality in professional science is competition, not just competition with men and its inherent strains on the female self-image, but especially competition among women. The contours and implications of this special problem of competing have yet to be fully understood (Keller & Moglen, 1987), but they nonetheless affect the experiences of many researchers.

Marginalization has been examined here as it has entailed the positioning of individual researchers and those workers' strategies to ensure survival and relative success, even when success did not include the training of a future generation of workers. Marginalization needs to be understood also in terms of the consequential fate of new ideas, for just as it has limited individual careers so it has influenced the intellectual work resulting from those careers. Potential curtailment of intellectual ideas extends beyond the neglect of the more radical feminist work mentioned earlier; our assessment of lost work must begin to include those risky ideas women dared not advance given their precarious professional standing, as well as those ideas set aside in order to become recognized as a stable and reliable researcher in a world where there is differential assessment of the work of men and women. Assessing these uncompleted projects, such as Leta Hollingworth's unfinished feminist magnum opus, *Miss Pilgrim's*

Progress, is not always possible, as the records of most of these ideas are lost forever (Agronick, 1988).

The philosophical seduction into the male rules of psychology has had another consequence for women's participation generally and feminist thinking in particular: *the denial of self-reflection*. The empiricist tradition assumes that the observer is a sensing conduit of observations; it makes no assumptions about the observer as a historical subject or rational agent (indeed, such conceptions usually have been taken to be antithetical to empiricism). Hence, self-reflection is thought to be inappropriate, unnecessary, or even impossible. Consistent with this epistemological rejection of self-reflection is the refusal to acknowledge *reflexivity*, the process and the results of our being both the subjects and objects in human research. To many nonempiricist social scientists, reflexive acts are seen as a rudiment of human functioning (Giddens, 1979, 39–40).

To comprehend the effects of the denial of self-reflection in psychology, it is necessary to examine the concept of reflexivity further. Historians of psychology have adopted the term reflexivity to refer to a process that is both inevitable—that is, we cannot engage in the production of psychological knowledge without it—and inadvertently consequential—that is, this basic reflecting influences the form and structure of knowledge. Buss (1978), for instance, has suggested that our unawareness of the reflexive process has resulted in a flip-flopping of theoretical models, an oscillation between theories based on the idea that the person constructs reality, that is, cognitive psychology, and those based on the idea that reality constructs the person, that is, behaviorism. The development of social psychology as a subdiscipline is tied to similar reflexive processes (Morawski, 1987). In brief, researchers' recognition of the complexities and irrationalities of social life (which had become apparent to them by the end of the nineteenth century) guided their construing of "social" in such a way that their own scientific practices were differentiated from the irrational and potentially explosive social forces of ordinary beings (Morawski, 1986).

The concept of reflexivity is also used in the sociology of science to refer to an intentional and metatheoretical process. In this context reflexivity is not taken to be inadvertent or unrecognized but an explicit operation in research. Oehler and Mullins (1986) suggest that reflexivity consists of two processes: "(1) an awareness on the part of research communities of the social bases of their theories and (2) some kind of institutional arrangement to encourage the development of that awareness and its public display" (2). Reflexivity of this sort is a self-critical operation and is aimed at improving research through critical analyses and corrective measures.

Probably because of its prescriptive adherence to natural science methods, psychology has not acknowledged reflexivity either as an inherent aspect of observing human action or as a self-conscious strategy of research. Thus it is not a simple matter to discuss how the denial of reflexivity has restricted the cognitive framework of women in psychology. When women psychologists have turned to the investigation of gender at least partly in order to understand their own place in modern society, their work has been restricted by the cognitive system that they entered—that is, empiricist psychology, like any epistemological worldview, is constituted by rules and axiomatic conditions that delimit experience in certain ways. Imbedded in the rules of empiricist psychology are categorical distinctions between reality and illusion, subjectivity and objectivity, rational and irrational, mind and body. Not only are these distinctions constitutive of empiricist psychology, but they are tied in basic ways to the governing arrangements of our social world; they are inextricably part of a system of patriarchal values.

There are at lest two distinct ways in which the denial of reflexivity—and by virtue of that, the cognitive contours of the dominant canon—have restricted women's work experiences, especially feminist research. First, the barriers against self-reflective thinking as an explicit and legitimate process has limited the incorporation of experiences and cognitive structurings that were more or less unique to women. It is difficult to specify exactly what has been lost as a consequence of these barriers precisely because of the unlikeliness that those experiences and cognitives ever have been given voice. There are occasions, however, where we can detect curtailment of such thinking; the following are two brief examples. One instance pertains to the efforts of some early twentieth-century women psychologists to unambiguously settle the question of the existence of psychological differences between the sexes. Many of these researchers utilized the scientific methods of the new psychology to design experiments on sex differences, but there was recognition among some of them, including the most enthusiastic experimenters, that these laboratory studies could not capture the *real* conditions of difference—that is, as feminists, they recognized sex differences as dependent on the entire social structure; no experiment could possibly control for the multitudinous effects of a discriminatory culture. Many researchers concurred on the ubiquitousness of differential treatment of males and females, yet they differed in their accommodation to this limitation in their empirical methods. Helen Thompson Wooley (1903) took a moderate stance: The introduction of her dissertation on the experimental study of sex differences contained a simple yet revealing caveat about the limits of her research. Wooley confessed that locating male and female subjects who had similar social experience and training "even in the most democratic community, is impossible" (2). She had to settle on using subjects from a coeducational college, the closest approximation to democratic conditions. Other psychologists were less resigned to the simple conceptualization of sex differences demanded by the experimental paradigm. Tanner (1896) claimed that "the real tendencies of women cannot be known until they are free to choose, any more than those of a tied up dog can be." To Tanner, the nature of sex differences "cannot be demonstrated until men and women are not only nominally free but actually free to enter any profession" (9–10). Not unlike the feminist utopists of the period, some researchers contemplated the perfect experiment: a social world in which men and women are treated equally (Peters, 1916). This is an instance where reflexive thinking could not be extended to the conventional paradigm. There are parallels in contemporary research: The various suggestions that laboratory procedures not only include sex bias but actually curtail the incorporation of women's experiences or cognitive frameworks has resulted in very few methodological changes (Lykes & Stewart, 1986).

Another example of barriers to reflexive thinking is necessarily more speculative for it concerns the abandonment of certain cognitive opportunities before they were developed. The substitution of empiricist techniques for feminist (and perhaps feminine) ones cannot simply entail a translation of interests but rather involves substantial shifts of interests. Professional training promised new but nevertheless different perspectives on reality than did feminist thinking. Phyllis Blanchard (1927) was one of the few who wrote about her acceptance of science over the radical feminism she had cultivated earlier:

> I had originally intended to write, but the drive to understand human motives and conduct, which arose out of the necessity of solving my own problems, developed into a desire to understand all behavior, and I turned to the social sciences. Probably this was a happy decision. Had I been only a writer, I might have prolonged indefinitely my separation from reality. Through a more scientific approach, I began to see things as they actually were rather than as I wished them to be. I even came to understand that in spite of the intensity of my feeling about marriage I might be able to accept the outward form so long as the inner spirit of the relationship embodied freedom. (473)

Blanchard celebrated the substitution of worldviews, but it remains that some beliefs, even if they were represented as a "separation from reality," were abandoned. The actual content of these lost ideas must remain largely a speculative question.

The denial of reflexivity has influenced women's participation in psychological research, then, through the exclusivity of the empiricist framework. Even when a researcher actively endorses empiricism, her work is restricted by certain categorical distinctions of that worldview. Thus, for instance, feminist psychologists who attempt to revise the conceptual distinction between sex and gender nevertheless actually reaffirm the existence of meaningful natural difference between males and females. It is not possible to discuss difference outside of an oppositional system that designates attributes as either natural or cultural. The attempts to reject the dichotomy of masculine and feminine have led to a similar impasse. Rejecting masculine and feminine categories in favor of an interactional one, androgyny, has in the process established a privileged signifier, the new he-woman/she-man that not only retains gender categories but in practice seems to give priority to the masculine underpinnings. The androgyny concept illustrates all too well that empiricist psychology cannot consider an unsteady state but is based on reified demarcations of reality. Although the concept of androgyny was constructed as a means to go beyond sex and gender categories, it is restrained by metatheoretical demarcations; therefore, for instance, androgyny is readily available to reabsorption as a *sexual* concept (Brown, 1986).

Researchers who attempt to expand the categorical structures of reality or transform the underlying dualisms encounter difficulties; empiricist reality is deeply structured by such dichotomies. Gilligan's (1982) development of a different moral thinking is interpreted as embracing traditional stereotypes about women (Colby & Damon, 1983). Even those researchers who are seemingly most faithful to empiricism in their efforts to appeal directly to the real world in order to analyze women's experiences cannot escape the categories; they end up creating psychological explanations that are tied inextricably to dualist categories and that recapitulate generic narratives of human causation, those revised yet classic tales of victims and heroines (Marks, 1985). Such studies thereby recreate scientifically sanctioned defenses of existing social arrangements and encourage the personal assimilation of these accounts.

Conventional psychology thus curtails self-reflective and critical opportunities. That science, however, is *reflexive*, and a number of feminist scholars have shown that what is reflected in the structure of science are social relations that are fitted to the experiences of men and a hierarchical social world. At the most visible level, images of science and of masculinity are mutually edifying: Both are signified through language as tough, rigorous, unemotional, rational, independent, competitive. This gender symbolism is now entrenched in contemporary psychology. Earlier in the century, however, the connections apparently required rehearsal. In the preface to the 1892 outline of a psychology course, Edmund Sanford reminded instructors that "the student of psychology must have its facts and principles brought home to him in a way not inferior to the best of other sciences, if psychology is to have the infusion of new vigor that they have had, and afford the healthy and virile training that they afford" (141). Writing on his advocation of serious experimental training, E. W. Scripture (1938) claimed that it would heighten cognitive and physical abilities; he encouraged the "education of men, instead of bookworms and mummies." Research "gets the mind into independent action, so that men become authorities and not echoes" (262). Manly images seem to have secured psychology its place as a real science.

Historians and philosophers of science have examined multiple forms of this gender symbolism. During the scientific revolution metaphors of gender were used to establish boundaries of truth and myth, the good and bad in knowledge seeking (Harding, 1986b; Keller, 1985; Merchant, 1980). Two aspects of this symbolism reveal how gender is reflected in contemporary science. First, the ideals and instrumental actions of science correspond to classic masculine psychology. Keller (1985) has elaborated how the social relations of scientific work—mastery, control, objectivity (observer separateness and distancing, individual-centered rationality)—are rooted in masculine attributes. Second, the development of gender symbolism in science resulted in epistemological categories that both mirrored and maintained gender arrangements in social life generally. The antimonies of rational-irrational, mind-body, cognitive-emotional, individual-social, active-passive reaffirmed stereotypic images of gender; they also served to protect the institution of science and its domination by men (Bleier, 1984; Fee, 1983; Keller, 1985). By privileging certain attributes and representing certain experiences, these dichotomies confirmed and reproduced a larger landscape of social relations.

Gender symbolism and male-centered presuppositions do not just inform how we code and describe observations in science, they also structure the entire process of knowledge seeking. Moulton (1983), for instance, has shown how the primary mode of communicating our ideas is adversarial: Our intellectual writings are offense maneuvers that aggressively pit a selected idea against that found in others' work. Through isolated and piecemeal attacks, the adversary method allows no means to question larger axioms of research, introduce novel systems, or engage in cooperative enterprises. Falsification, though not simply in Popper's sense of the term, is what we do to each others' work. Similarly, Flax (1983) has analyzed how dualistic categories of mind and body, subject and object, are more than surface symbols. Using object-relations theory, Flax suggested that these dichotomies represent the problematizing of "others" that is part of normal male development. Linguistic analyses, conducted primarily by literary theorists, demonstrate how our discourse also mirrors, structures, and reproduces social relations. Jardine (1985) has analyzed the writings of modern French philosophers to ascertain the process through which they bring woman into their texts. Sedgwick (1985) has examined homosociality in nineteenth-century literature, elucidating the multiple ways in which relations between men structure power relations between men and women. Using a text more familiar to psychologists, Steele (1987) has analyzed a paper by a foremost personality theorist, showing how cognition and reason are placed above critical scrutiny, as well as how the writing suggests latent fears associated with childhood, castration, and women.

These historical, philosophical, and literary studies indicate how gender and gender relations are reflected in knowledge structures. They intimate the third consequence of the seduction of empiricism in psychology: the *reproduction of social relations* of power. Knowledge structures are comprised of normative social relations and generally sustain these relations. Therefore, working as empiricists necessarily entails an affirmation of particular relations. The human relations constitutive of empiricist science are now being analyzed: They include not simply those relations between workers within a discipline or across disciplines, but also the relations established through the very demarcation between science and society and between what is taken as the observers and the subjects of observation. Not only are researchers members of communities governed by rules of membership and exclusion, but work arrangements and hierarchies influence their products. From a more macrosocial perspective, advances in science can be seen as displacing existing social arrangements and introducing new relations—including the relations between scientists, the organisms under study, government, consumers (Foucault, 1970; Latour, 1983). Social transformations in scientific work thus affect the apparent borders between science and society, as well as the structures and production of scientific communities.

The case of androgyny research illustrates the reproduction of social relations in empiricist work. The introduction of the concept of androgyny was not entirely revolutionary, for it actually represents the continuation of a shift in authorial control over the supposed realm of masculinity and femininity. In the early decades of this century, psychologists had worked to demonstrate the existence of gender attributes and then to establish their special relation to them—that is, conceptual definitions were developed along with psychometric devices that indicated that masculinity and femininity could be detected only by the specially trained psychologist; even the subjects themselves could not identify their femininity or masculinity (Morawski, 1985). The creation of the androgyny concept shifted these relations further: The critiques of masculinity-femininity research indicated that conventional developmental and personality psychologists evaluated gender traits inaccurately and that feminist-informed researchers were better prepared to make evaluations. Just as the construction of androgyny research credited a new group of researchers and created a new source of work, so it also posited a promising identity for professional women scientists (who were becoming the majority of researchers on gender). The androgyny concept offered new social roles that supplanted older, certainly derogatory, images of the female scientist, the woman who thinks like a man, with a more becoming form of gendered personality, the independent woman worker who is also gentle and receptive. Androgyny research altered more than the social relations among certain scientific workers: It afforded a new expert perspective on society. It reconfirmed that psychological science commands a penetrating gaze on popular life in that androgyny research presumably could locate, identify, and dissect such (potent and confusing) cultural phenomena as acceptable cross dressing, businesswomen, Boy George, gentle men, and Annie Lennox of the Eurythmics.

Although androgyny research illustrates the multiple social relations that are maintained through research, the example should not be taken as indicating that gender research has been particularly powerful in altering social relations. As discussed earlier, we must remain mindful of the fact that gender research in psychology has had limited audiences and participants.

Psychology and Feminist Epistemology

The seduction and entrance into a logical empiricist household has not eliminated the marginality of women participants, a primary goal of feminist empiricism. Nor has that environment been conducive to self-critical reflexive thought, a process feminists have relied on both to understand the intricacies of sexism and to generate visions of new systems. Rather, empiricist science takes the male gaze as the natural perspective and continues to place women as the problematized Other. The antimonies of empiricism lend validity to certain descriptions of reality and disadvantage other accounts. Likewise, particular social relations in science are sustained and nurtured.

The concept of gender remains entangled in this social system. As a subject of analysis, gender is understood through categorical dualisms. Like an unhappy household, social relations that are undesirable for the women who are participating are somehow reproduced. Scientific knowledge, then, needs to be understood as *social* power, not as a universal commodity or parcel of truth statements. Once science is understood in social and relational terms, the practical opportunities for feminist research can be explored. Before entertaining these possibilities, however, we need to gain some analytic purchase on the cognitive and epistemological choices available to feminist researchers—choices that include options of transforming empiricism.

As we have seen, feminists' engagement with empiricist psychology has created opportunities of two sorts: a foundation for the critique of bias, and a legitimate system for investigating women's lives. Yet the costs of these engagements have been substantial in that feminist empiricist studies (and women workers) typically have been designated as marginal. The potential of empiricism is limited by the gendered nature of its precepts, a worldview sustained by dualities related to gender. Returning to Riemer's (1986) notion of the philosophical seduction of the daughter, the conflicts within feminist empiricism reflect an inevitable tension between the allegiance to a discourse of the father and a feminist discourse of discontent.

The tension in a feminist psychology that adheres to empiricism has repeatedly led to impasses in research programs, but such paralysis is not necessary. In fact, it can be seen as the first of several steps leading to a feminist transformation of discourse (Riemer, 1986). The next step requires further separation from the master discourse and the need to both identify desired values and engage in more explicit deconstruction of that discourse. In the past two decades, in the psychology of gender there have been gestures to make these moves. Weisstein's (1971) prescient unpacking of the sexist values underlying scientific psychology afforded a framework for further critical analysis. Parlee's (1979) review of the psychology of women provided an enlightened account of the need to generate theories that recognized social power as central to understanding women's actions. Kessler and McKenna (1978) developed a promising theoretical model that suggested that gender is not so much an intrinsic object or traits but rather a phenomenological process. A handful of other similar works could be mentioned, but it remains that little has become of the efforts to establish new values and precepts or to present comprehensive critiques of the master discourse.

One means to confront this apparent impasse in psychology is to consider areas where feminists have generated new values for scientific knowledge seeking. Harding's (1986b) taxonomy, although somewhat general, suggests two other existing frameworks for feminist science. The feminist standpoint is represented by several different theories including socialist and cultural feminism, which all share the claim that women's material experiences privilege their understanding of the world. Although its universalizing of women is problematic, work within the feminist standpoint has made valuable contributions to imagining alternative epistemologies. This scholarship has articulated the ways in which the life experiences of women afford a different view of the world and has indicated how these experiences are constructed and constrained by the predominant social structure. From these accounts, the feminist standpoint has enabled a clarification of alternative values and visions of the world, that is, relational thinking, connectedness with others and nature, the function and meaning of reproductive processes. By attending to the relation between experiences and social structure, work within the feminist standpoint has delineated the processes whereby social relations of power are maintained and reproduced at a psychological level.

The other framework described by Harding (1986b) actually developed through other, largely nonfeminist movements: Feminist postmodernism assembles many of the features of postmodernism. Perhaps the chief feature is a general disclaiming of the search for enduring, absolute, or universal truths; these dubitable truths include the existence of a stable, autonomous knower, the possibility of objective, disinterested knowledge, the existence of logic, rationality, or reason that is independent of a social system endorsing those mental processes, and the feasibility of referential language to describe reality. In addition to the deconstructive or critical features, feminist postmodernism has fostered various proposals for alternative conceptions of truth, progress, and knowledge making. Among these generative possibilities for new metatheory are the recognition of identity (and, hence, the knower) as fragmented, plural, and conflicted; and the recognition that models of knowledge and truth are contingent on social relations, historical context, and the knower's interests. In these works, language and social relations become central to the production of knowledge, to the representation of experience. Knowledge is recognized as necessarily pragmatic and partial and the role of the knower as inherently social and political (Flax, 1987).

A brief overview does not properly elucidate the complexities and variations within these two frameworks. It likewise fails to indicate the problems and contradictions contained in these epistemologies (for a detailed analysis, see Harding, 1986b).

What should be recognized is that the models are formative and plural; they are not even necessarily mutually exclusive. In fact, some of the most promising feminist analyses of science have drawn from both perspectives. Affirming the unique experiences of women, Fee (1983), for instance, argues that this affirmative feminist position enables a critique of male-created illusions about science, myths such as the antinomies of objectivity and subjectivity, thinking and feeling, and science and society. Fee (1986) suggests that just as we comprehend science as constituted through particular social relations and hierarchies, so we must understand that critiques of science result from different social relations (of race, class, gender); therefore, an alternative science is dependent on a variety of critiques of domination. In a somewhat different amalgamation of socialist feminism and postmodernism, Haraway (1985) proposes that the feminist struggles with science and technology be reconstructed by embracing the partiality and contradictions of knowledge along with our fractured and unclosed identities. Even Harding (1986a) has utilized more than one of these epistemological frameworks in her recommendations for feminist theorizing.

These epistemologies are not presented here as ready-made alternatives for empiricism, they also contain male-biased axioms. What they illustrate, however, is the existence of other feasible responses to the three core inquiries of epistemology: how we can know anything, the process whereby a subject can acquire knowledge; what it is that can be known, usually framed as the question of the nature of reality; and how knowledge is validated, the procedures and proof structures for certifying knowledge. Translated into everyday terms of "doing psychology," the responses to these questions inform our working assumptions about the observer's capacities as well as the subject's actions. They determine what is to count as sound methods, reputable results, or an adequate theory. These are precisely the questions that cannot be examined seriously from the position of feminist empiricism. Yet once science is understood as social relations (both in the sense of being constituted by particular social relations and maintaining particular social relations), the importance of exploring these questions become obvious. Writings of the feminist standpoint and postmodernism indicate how knowledge is produced *within*, *through*, and *for* certain social relations.

Feminist empiricist research in psychology has illustrated the tenacity of these social relations, especially through the gendered nature of knowledge production and the binds of reflexivity. But that research tradition also can teach us strategies for altering social relations and ultimately its associated epistemological foundations—that is, the unfortunate experiences of using empiricist practices can inform us about alternative strategies; they signal when and where working within conventional practices will not work. They demonstrate that feminists cannot rely on abstract, universal proof structures and presumptions about some incorrigible audience of reasonable and unbiased empiricists. Likewise, the experiences of feminist psychologists highlight the limits of some of our social relations of work: marginality, isolation, and limited prospects for generating new researchers. These experiences, coupled with a social-relational understanding of science, can guide the construction of new epistemologies through the imagination and testing of different work practices.

Feminist Psychology and Practice

How might feminism in psychology influence the normative constituents of knowledge making? This question is best approached by considering in turn each of the three core features of epistemology: who is the knower, what can be known, and how knowledge is established. Replacement of the traditional positivist account of these features can be guided by the experiences of women in science. The search need not, in fact should not, be expected to result in another abstract epistemological code of conduct; the consequences of women's seduction and adherence to such codes stand as a lesson well learned. By addressing each of the core features and attending to the tensions produced by various recipes for their preparation, we might instead contemplate practices that recognize and constructively utilize tensions and contradictions. We can benefit by the often painful awareness of how social relations of power are reproduced in professional practices as well as personal life. Such awareness makes it possible to find new meanings in scientific activities, say, in a colleague's allegiance to professional or institutional rules. With this recognition we can develop strategies that challenge and eventually transform those rules of appropriate scientific activity. The strategic practices implied here are really the core of my thinking about where feminist efforts might be most needed and, hopefully, most effective. A personal understanding of how social relations structure *who* and *what* counts as valid and authentic, not to mention worthy and laudable, is an essential prerequisite to altering those relations of power.

Feminist scholarship has repeatedly demonstrated that how and what we come to know depends on *who* we are. The conception of an adequate knower bequeathed to us from the Enlightenment philosophies is rational, reasonable, removed from the physical context of body, time, and place; that knower is gendered male. These gendered conceptions of the ideal knower attest to what women social scientists have learned by virtue of their professional marginality: We are *situated knowers*, located within a dynamic social structure. It has become apparent that knowing is *relational*, that it is dependent on the person's participation and position within a community of would-be knowers. Knowing also is *historical*: it is a transitory process dependent on one's location within a temporally bound context. Finally, *reflexivity*, both phenomenal and critical, is instrumental to how we know. These observations on knowing break with the traditional axiom that the knower is separate from what is known. They nicely imply that inconsistencies and instabilities in knowing are not necessarily error but are no more or less than the consequence of the fact that knowing bodies exist in specific places, times, and social circumstances. Knowing is no less valid in this conception, and the tentativeness as well as partiality of the knower and knowing become a potential in the generation of new knowledge.

The exploration of women's particular positions as knowers within the Western philosophic tradition stands as a case in point. Women's knowing has often been referred to as a double viewing: a bifurcated consciousness where we see in two different ways, as participating agents in intellectual work and as marginalized observers (as scientists and as women). Double viewing marks our situation as fractured historical identities, as actors and subjects in the social relations of science. It disrupts the conception of scientists as autonomous individuals.

Feminist studies have revealed with equal clarity the gendered nature of what is known. Just within the program of feminist empiricism exists a strong indictment of the subject of modern psychology. Historical analysis of educational philosophy reveals that the entire Western tradition of learning presupposes not only masculine forms of learning but of what is to be learned: Education concerns the productive world of knowing but not the reproductive (Martin, 1985). The reality we have sought to know is gendered in fundamental ways. Critical studies of the social sciences, which include not only feminist analyses, have located a latent Other behind all objects of inquiry; typically that other is the feminine (or nonwhite, non-European). The identification of this presupposed other forces a more candid admission that the final object of knowing is the *self* or selves. Thus, even when inquiry focuses on some object distinct from oneself, that object is made real by virtue of its relation to self; it is a matter of *difference*.

At least two strategies emerge from these reformulations of the knowing subject and the object of knowledge. First, an under-

standing of the reflective, relational, and temporal consciousness of the knower and of the knower's relation to what is to be
known suggests that there is no single identity of knowers. Thus, as
an epistemological issue, the question of the object of inquiry is
transformed. Knowledge seeking can be seen as an activity under-
taken by historical and fractured identities to recover what is latent
or hidden from our known reality. This needs to be seen as a positive
transformation enabling us to work with more dynamic relations
between what was taken as the subject and object of knowing. It is
generative in that it offers more possibilities for the form and outcome of inquiries. In turn, these inquiries can and must incorporate
what has been omitted: the conscious experiences of the inquiries,
especially those experiences that reflect contradictions, denial, for-
getting, and our implications in modern institutions.

Second, recognition of fractured identities and nonautono-
mous knowers also affords new strategies for reformulating psychological research. What has been identified as women's bifurcated vision illustrates this potential: If used consciously, double
viewing disrupts the clear narrative of science. That narrative,
which has served to guide truth seeking and to validate certain
truth claims, ceases to be either cohesive or comprehensive.
Multifocal seeing enables recognition of tensions and contradictions. Such viewing also renders the rhetoric of science more
transparent, making apparent that what we *say* and *write* about
scientific activities is an important part of scientific work.

These possible strategies intimate the key issues involved in
the question of appropriate means for validating knowledge
claims. Once the distinction between knower and knowledge is
rejected, the criteria for what counts as adequate knowledge or
truth must be substantially modified, since traditional criteria
serve the ideals of separateness, disinterestedness, control, and
manipulation (all of which depend on the motion of an autonomous knower who is separate from the object). The generation of
new rules for adequate knowledge will depend on the particular
reworking of subject and object relations. The reformulations

and strategies we have discussed do indicate some core features of such guidelines. First, standards of research will necessarily be *pluralist*, enabling different researchers or research communities to produce knowledge that is sensitive to the context and history of the specific subject as well as the identities of the researchers themselves. Just as we have recognized that gender cannot have the same meaning or consequences for women of all races and classes at all times, so observational statements might be assessed from a compatible pluralist perspective. Perhaps, for instance, we might experiment with assessing the affinity of observational statements rather than the older criterion of correspondence or identity. Related to pluralist standards is the necessity of flexible and revisable rules of research; indeed, the strategies proposed begin with a challenge of the validity of conventional rules. Even aside from feminist scholarship, it has been shown that psychology has demonstrated an unbecoming rigidity in its adherence to abstract, unquestioned rules for validating knowledge (Leahey, 1980). Thus, for instance, feminist recognition of contradictions and inconsistencies in knowledge claims offers a basis for proposing intelligibility as a more adequate guide to work standards than the conventional expectations of comprehensiveness or generality (Shortland, 1986). Finally, *language* is a serious concern, not only in terms of the function of narratives in making and confirming scientific claims, but also in disclosing multiple identities in science. In science, conversations of persuasion traditionally have advantaged masculine performances (Moulton, 1983) and have privileged certain voices in the hierarchy of research communities (Addleson, 1983). The actual and possible uses of language, then, must be a primary consideration in restructuring the evaluation of research.

Toward Practice

Thinking about transformed proof structures moves us toward the speculative. Although speculation and fantasy are crucial to feminist movements (Caplan, 1987; Morawski, 1988b), the argument underlying my analysis of strategies is that it all depends on practice, on what we do. In order to overcome the impasses of empiricism it is necessary that we alter our work practices and construct new social relations along with the new scientific narratives (Fee, 1986; Haraway, 1986; Mies, 1983). Given that scientific practices are comprised simply of ordinary and everyday actions, a feminist psychology depends on a reflexive vigilance over what we do in our day-to-day lives as feminist scientists. We need to monitor our ordinary actions as scientists, noting where these actions align themselves with science, which has been gendered male. And we need to guide our actions to disrupt and reconstruct these gender-coded alignments. If we can change how we evaluate a colleague's work (or our own), initiate cooperative activities, consider the significance of solidarity, and give voice to our subjectivities and unspoken experiences, then we can continue work on a feminist science.

REFERENCES

Addleson, K. P. (1983). The man of professional wisdom. In S. Harding and M. B. Hintikka (Eds.), *Discovering reality: Feminist perspectives on epistemology, metaphysics, methodology, and philosophy of science* (165–86). Boston: Reidel.

Agronick, G. (1988). *Feminist psychologists, 1915–1930: Personal, political, and professional constraints.* B.A. Thesis, Wesleyan University.

Bem, S. L. (1974). The measurement of psychological androgyny. *Journal of Consulting and Clinical Psychology, 42,* 155–62.

Blanchard, P. (1927). The long journey. *Nation, 124,* 472–73.

Bleier, R. (1984). *Science and gender: A critique of biology and its theories on women.* New York: Pergamon Press.

Brown, R. (1986). *Social psychology, the second edition.* New York: Free Press.

Buss, H. R. (1978). The structure of scientific revolutions. *Journal of the History of the Behavioral Sciences, 14,* 57–64.

Caplan, C. (1987). The thorn birds: Fiction, fantasy, femininity. In C. Caplan, *Sea changes* (117–46). London: Verso.

Colby, A. & Damon, W. (1983). Listening to a different voice: A review of Giligan's "in a different voice". *Merrill-Palmer Quarterly, 29*, 473–81.

Deaux, K. & Major, B. (1987). Putting gender into context: An interactive model of gender-related behavior. *Psychological Review, 94*, 369–89.

Eagly, A. H. (1978). Sex differences in influenceability. *Psychological Bulletin, 85*, 86–116.

Eagly, A. H. (1987). *Sex differences in social behavior: A social role interpretation.* Hillsdale, NJ: Erlbaum.

Fausto-Sterling, A. (1985). *Myths of gender: Biological theories about women and men.* New York: Basic Books.

Fee, E. (1983). Women's nature and scientific objectivity. In M. Lowe & R. Hubbard (Eds.), *Woman's nature: Rationalization of inequality* (9–28). New York: Pergamon Press.

Fee, E. (1986). Critiques of modern science: The relationship of feminism to other radical epistemologies. In R. Bleier (Ed.), *Feminist approaches to science* (42–56). New York: Pergamon Press.

Fisher, B. (1988). Wandering in the wilderness: The search for women role models. *Signs, 13*, 211–33.

Flax, J. (1987). Postmodernism and gender relations in feminist theory. *Signs, 12*, 621–43.

Flax, J. (1983). Political philosophy and the patriarchal unconscious: A psychoanalytic perspective on epistemology and metaphysics. In S. Harding & M. B. Hintikka (Eds.), *Discovering reality: Feminist perspectives on epistemology, metaphysics, methodology, and philosophy of science* (245–282). Boston: Reidel.

Foucault, M. (1970). *The order of things: An archeology of the human sciences.* New York: Random House.

Furumoto, L. (1988). Shared knowledge: The experimentalists, 1904–1929. In J. G. Morawski (Ed.), *The rise of experimentation in American psychology* (94–113). New Haven: Yale University Press.

Giddens, A. (1979). *Central problems in social theory.* Berkeley: University of California Press, 1979.

Gilligan, C. (1982). *In a different voice: Psychological theory and women's development.* Cambridge, MA: Harvard University Press.

Glazer, P. M. & Slater, M. (1987). *Unequal colleagues: The entrance of women into the professions, 1890–1940.* New Brunswick: Rutgers University Press.

Gubar, S. (1981). Blessings in disguise: Cross-dressing as re-dressing for female modernists. *Massachusetts Review, 22*, 477–508.

Haaken, J. (1988). Field dependence research: A historical analysis of a psychological construct. *Signs, 13*, 311–30.

Haraway, D. (1985). A manifesto for cyborgs: Science, technology, and socialist feminism in the 1980s. *Socialist Review, 15*, 65–107.

Haraway, D. (1986). Primatology is politics by other means. In R. Bleier (Ed.), *Feminist approaches to science* (77–118). New York: Pergamon Press.

Harding, S. (1986a). The instability of the analytical categories of feminist theory. *Signs, 11*, 645–64.

Harding, S. (1986b). *The science question in feminism.* Ithaca, NY: Cornell University Press.

Jardine, A. A. (1985). *Gynesis: Configurations of woman and modernity.* Ithaca, NY: Cornell University Press.

Keller, E. F. (1985). *Reflections on gender and science.* New Haven: Yale University Press.

Keller, E. F. & Moglen, H. (1987). Competition and feminism: Conflicts for academic women. *Signs, 12*, 493–511.

Kessler, S. J. & McKenna, W. (1978). *Gender: An ethnomethodological approach.* New York: Wiley.

Lakoff, R. (1975). *Language and woman's place.* New York: Harper.

Latour, B. (1983). Give me a laboratory and I will raise the world. In R. Knorr-Cetina & M. Mulkay (Eds.), *Science observed* (141–70). Berkeley: Sage.

Leahey, T. (1980). The myth of operationism. *Journal of Mind and Behavior, 1*, 127–43.

Lykes, M. B. & Stewart, A. J. (1986). Evaluating the feminist challenge in psychology: 1963–1983. *Psychology of Women Quarterly, 11*, 393–411.

Marks, E. (1985). Feminism's wake. *Boundary Two, 14*, 99–111.

Martin, J. R. (1985). *Reclaiming a conversation: The ideal of the educated woman.* New Haven: Yale University Press.

McClone, J. (1980). Sex differences in human brain asymmetry: A critical survey. *Behavioral and Brain Sciences, 3*, 215–63.

Merchant, C. (1980). *The death of nature: Women, ecology, and the scientific revolution.* New York: Harper & Row.

Mies, M. (1983). Towards a methodology for feminist research. In G. Bowles & R. D. Klein (Eds.), *Theories of women's studies* (117–39). London: Routledge and Kegan Paul.

Morawski, J. G. (1985). The measurement of masculinity and femininity: Engendering categorical realities. *Journal of Personality, 53*, 196–223.

Morawski, J. G. (1986). Contextual discipline: The unmaking and remaking of sociality. In R. L. Rosnow & M. Georgoudi (Eds.),

Contextualism and understanding in behavioral science (47–66). New York: Praeger.

Morawski, J. G. (1987). The troubled quest for masculinity, femininity and androgyny. *Review of Personality and Social Psychology, 7,* 44–69.

Morawski, J. G. (1988a). Impossible experiments and practical constructions: The social bases of psychologists' work. In J. G. Morawski (Ed.), *The rise of experimentation in American psychology* (72–930). New Haven: Yale University Press.

Morawski, J. G. (1988b). Impasse in feminist thought? In M. M. Gergen (Ed.), *Feminist structures of knowledge* (182–94). New York: New York University Press.

Moulton, J. (1983). A paradigm of philosophy: The adversary method. In S. Harding & M. B. Hintikka (Eds.), *Discovering reality: feminist perspectives on epistemology, metaphysics, methodology, and philosophy of science* (149–161). Boston: Reidel.

Oehler, K. & Mullins, N. C. (1986). *Mechanisms of reflexivity in science: A look at nontraditional literary forms.* Paper presented at the meetings of the Society for the Social Studies of Science, Pittsburgh, October 1986.

Parlee, M. B. (1973). The premenstrual syndrome. *Psychological Bulletin, 80,* 454–65.

Parlee, M. B. (1979). Psychology and women. *Signs, 5,* 121–33.

Parlee, M. B. (1982). Changes in moods and activation levels during the menstrual cycle in experimentally naive subjects. *Psychology of Women Quarterly, 7,* 119–31.

Peters, I. L. (1916). A questionnaire study of some of the effects of social restrictions on the American girl. *Peddagogical Seminary, 23,* 550–69.

Riemer, R. (1986). Political thought: A re-visioning. *Women and Politics, 6,* 5–67.

Rosenberg, R. L. (1982). *Beyond separate spheres: Intellectual origins of modern feminism.* New Haven: Yale University Press.

Rossiter, M. W. (1982). *Women scientists in America: Struggles and strategies to 1940.* Baltimore: Johns Hopkins University Press.

Sanford, E. C. (1892). A laboratory course in physiological psychology. *American Journal of Psychology, 4,* 141–55.

Scarborough, E. & Furumoto, L. (1987). *Untold lives: The first generation of American women psychologists.* New York: Columbia University Press.

Scripture, E. W. (1936). E. W. Scripture. In C. Murchison (Ed.), *The history of psychology in autobiography* (Vol. 3, 231–62). Worcester, MA: Clark University Press.

Sedgwick, E. K. (1985). *Between men: English literature and male homosocial desire.* New York: Columbia University Press.

Shortland, M. (1986). Bodies of history: Some problems and perspectives. *History of Science, 24,* 303–26.

Smith-Rosenberg, C. (1985). *Disorderly conduct: Visions of gender in Victorian America.* New York: Knopf.

Steele, R. S. (1987). *A critical hermeneutics for psychology: Beyond positivism to an exploration of the textual unconscious.* Unpublished manuscript, Wesleyan University.

Stewart, A. J. (1980). Personality and situation in the prediction of women's life patterns. *Psychology of Women Quarterly, 5,* 195–206.

Striegel-Moore, R. H., Silberstein, L. R. & Rodin, J. (1986). Toward an understanding of risk factors for bulimia. *American Psychologist, 41,* 246–63.

Tanner, A. (1896). The community of ideas of men and women. *Psychological Review, 3,* 549–50.

Thompson, H. B. (1903). *The mental traits of sex.* Chicago: University of Chicago Press.

Thorne, B. & Henley, N. (Eds.). (1975) *Language and sex: Difference and dominance.* Rowley, MA: Newbury House.

Trigg, M. (1987). *The characterization of herself: Lorine Pruette on women, men, and marriage in the 1920s.* Paper presented at the Berkshire Conference on the History of Women.

Weisstein, N. (1971). Psychology constructs the female. In V. Gornick & B. K. Moran (Eds.), *Woman in sexist society* (207–224). New York: Signet.

Wittenstein, K. (1987). *Beatrice M. Hinkle and the feminist use of psychoanalysis, 1910–1930.* Paper presented at the Berkshire Conference on the History of Women.

Wooley, H. B. T. (1903). *The mental traits of sex: An experimental investigation of the normal mind in men and women.* Chicago: University of Chicago Press.

6

Beyond Difference

RACHEL T. HARE-MUSTIN AND JEANNE MARECEK

A map is not the territory.

—Korzybski

The categories of male and female have been central to Western thought, entering virtually every domain of human experience and structuring human relationships. Gender categories serve to label, define, and rank. Gender also serves as a metaphor invoked to explain variations in human endeavors and human entitlements.

Like the culture of which it is part, the discipline of psychology also has used gender categories to organize human experience, as well as to define and rank individuals. Psychological theory and research have promoted the readiness of Western society to perceive its members as males and females rather than as individuals. Further, psychology has promulgated the notion that gender differences are attributes residing within individuals, like fortunes within fortune cookies, rather than behaviors arising from social relationships involving power and desire.

In this book we contend that such categories as masculine and feminine are abstractions, signifiers for the ways that men and women are in relation with one another. As abstractions, such categories are removed from the specific behaviors that give rise to them. This separation from specific behavior obscures the extent to which gender relations are relations of power. Although gender has other meanings as well, its meaning as power is crucial. Moreover, the inequities of power between men and women are often concealed in our culture.

Drawing attention to inequality in male-female relations arouses considerable cultural resistance. In American society, egalitarianism is a primary value. Americans are thus strongly disposed to deny relations of inequality. Moreover, those who have power in such an "egalitarian" society have a vested interest in either denying their privileged position or legitimizing it as natural, moral, or right. Instances of such denial are commonplace. In the nineteenth century, for example, the ideal of shielding women from sexual knowledge ensured female subservience to male sexual desires. Nowadays, women's sexual subservience is legitimated by what Wendy Hollway (1984) and others have labeled the male sex-drive discourse, the cultural belief that men have a barely controllable physiological need for sexual gratification. The legitimation of male power can also be seen when violent husbands justify their abusive behavior as disciplining their wives for infractions of household rules or as punishment for poor housekeeping or neglectful childcare (Gordon, 1988). At a more general level, we suggest that psychology's emphasis on the differences between men and women also has supported the unwarranted scientific legitimization of masculine privilege.

Difference: Complementarity or Asymmetry?

The focus on difference in gender theorizing reflects the tendency of traditional Western epistemology to dichotomize experience by imposing symmetry on nonsymmetrical relationships. Thus, classic gender-role theories have portrayed male and female roles as opposite, complementary, reciprocal, and equal. These theories imbue gender relations with a pseudo-mutuality; domination is made to appear no more serious than a game played equally by both parties (MacKinnon & Miller, 1987). One of the central tenets of classic gender-role theories is the idea of a complementary division of labor in family and society, rooted in the supposedly natural roles of male and female in sexuality and reproduction.

The notions of dichotomy, complementarity, equality, and reciprocity in gender roles and in the division of labor by sex can all be disputed. The division of labor in contemporary society assigns women the domestic task of promoting family welfare and men the task of producing income. This division is the basis for separate public and private spaces associated with men and women, as well as for status differences between men and women. Yet, the cultural ideals of individuality, independence, and achievement pertain only to accomplishments in the public sphere, not to endeavors in the private sphere. Thus, by situating men in the public sphere, the division of labor favors men's attainment of those cultural ideals. The accepted division of labor recruits and employs women's labor in the service of helping men attain those ideals. The designations "two-person careers" and "greedy occupations" refer to jobs in which a husband's success requires the unrecognized and unpaid efforts of his wife in addition to his own (Handy, 1978; Papanek, 1973). They suggest how wives are recruited to promote men's occupational success. More generally, women's invisible family work often makes possible what is seen as men's independence and autonomy (Hare-Mustin & Marecek, 1986). In sum, the conventional division of labor does not provide men and women with equivalent opportunities for culturally defined success. The efforts that women contribute toward their husbands' successes are yet to be widely reciprocated.

We can also challenge the myth that conventional gender roles are complementary. The idea that women's association with the domestic sphere is a natural and inevitable product of their biological function, and the assumption that domestic labor is all that women do, are both readily disputed by labor force statistics. Indeed, both in traditional agrarian societies and in modern capitalist societies, women are—and have always been—substantial contributors to the income-generating activities of their households. Women carry the burden of family welfare and household maintenance *in addition to* generating income. This is a burden that men by and large do not share; moreover, they often lack the skills to do so.

Rather than denying that inequality prevails, as ideas of gender-role complementarity do, we need to acknowledge it. We can then explore its contours in depth. The subordinate position that women hold in the gender hierarchy serves as the infrastructure of the hierarchy. What is marginalized and concealed by the myth of a complementary division of labor and the cultural belief in female inferiority is women's place at the center of the family and the social system (Hare-Mustin, 1988).

Another unacknowledged aspect of the asymmetry in gender roles is women's dual socialization. Women live out their lives in both the dominant male culture and the female subculture. This dual experience provides women with the potential of *double vision*, a dual perspective on the world. Thus, women have the possibility of seeing "as a woman" as well as seeing "as a man." In this respect, the customary hierarchy of male superiority-female inferiority is inverted. In theorizing gender, some feminists have attempted to make use of this double vision to gain new knowledge (e.g., Brown, 1989; Hartsock, 1985; Reinharz, 1985; Smith, 1979). We echo Jill Morawski's invitation to use this double vision to explore contradictions between culturally accepted wisdom and what we experience as outsiders, to disrupt conventional categories of knowledge and to reenvision what has been taken for granted.

RECONSTRUCTING GENDER

A central theme of this book is the reconstruction of gender. Humans have created gender by linking social behaviors and expectations to sexual specialization, but we cannot readily comprehend what we have created. To comprehend fully a system of which one is a part is impossible. Gender is so fundamental to Western thinking that its meaning escapes our attention. The difficulty in grasping the meaning of gender is compounded by the pervasive cultural belief that we have not created gender, but that gender is natural and largely explained by the biological differences of males and females. When we associate gender merely with sexual differences, gender itself becomes construed as difference, and gender differences are therefore also seen as natural. Thus, the politics of gender is the politics of difference.

Many feminists have taken issue with received wisdom about an essential female nature and have been courageous and forthright in drawing attention to the need for social change. In the discipline of psychology, feminist attention to gender has furnished a valuable corrective to outdated and blatantly prejudiced findings regarding women and gender. Also, as Bernice Lott points out, feminist psychologists have succeeded in expanding the scholarly focus from explanations invoking biological (and hence seemingly immutable) attributes to those invoking learned traits and behaviors. Feminist psychologists have also succeeded in shifting attention from an exclusive focus on difference and dichotomy to an expanded focus on similarity and overlap in characteristics of women and men. The contributions that feminists have made have been formidable, and it is not our intention to minimize them. Yet we also must note that feminist psychologists' work on gender issues thus far mostly fits within the conventional framework of focusing on gender differences. As Jill Morawski points out, the cultural construction of gender has disciplined our imagination.

Although the psychological study of gender fits within a conventional frame, its cumulative effects are to strain this frame. A crucial aspect of feminist work is that it has problematized gender. Feminists have gained a significant voice in defining gender to the public at large. Although the feminist voice is not the only voice, and feminist pronouncements are far from unitary and undisputed, many feminist ideas about male and female provide a counterpoint to traditional views. Critical scholarship and revisionist research by feminist psychologists have raised skepticism about facile assertions of either difference or no difference. Casting doubt on what had previously been undisputed is a crucial step toward opening the conversation about the meaning of gender.

We hope that the essays in this book have served as a next step. We believe that it is time for a paradigm shift in psychological theorizing on gender. We find it curious that psychological thought is still heavily influenced by such nineteenth-century theorists as Darwin, Marx, and Freud. As products of their era, they were primarily supportive of the status quo, of upper-class white male privilege with its limited knowledge of and marginal concern for women. If they were alive today, they would be astonished: What? You are still using those old books? Throw them away!

RECONSTRUCTING PSYCHOLOGY

Another theme of this book is the connection between reconstructing gender and reconstructing psychology. Feminist philosophers and historians have been important participants in movements aimed at transforming the natural and social sciences (cf. Haraway, 1983, 1989; Crawford & Marecek, 1989; Harding, 1986; Keller, 1985; Rose, 1983). They have helped lay bare shortcomings in such scientific dogmas as the separation of knowledge and values, the ideal of objectivity, and the image of science as an institution existing above and apart from society, invariably noble in its purposes, beneficial in its results.

The feminist critique in psychology has pointed out pervasive biases in psychological research and in the theories that the research has supported and forwarded. The psychology of individual differences, for example, has promoted the idea of the individual as an autonomous, self-determining agent separate from the surrounding context and even transcending social institutions. As we have pointed out in chapter 2, the construction of the self in Western thought is not neutral, but derives from male experience. Ultimately, for women "to be included in the big 'one' means not to be equally represented, but to be unrepresented, . . . to be swallowed up whole, negated in the quest for assimilation" (Keller, 1987, 276).

In attempting to eliminate the biases in psychological research, feminist psychologists have devised any number of creative methodological innovations. But each improvement has revealed yet more sources of bias. This suggests that bias is linked not only to the prevailing gender prejudice but also to underlying flaws in the guiding epistemology of psychologists. Conventional wisdom in psychology, for example, draws a sharp distinction between theory and method in research. Methods are construed as neutral tools that can be applied to the investigation of any aspect of the natural and social world. But a method is not neutral and it is not a mere tool. To have a method, as Gadamer (1976) says, is to have an interpretation. The method of inquiry determines what can be found.

Behind any method of acquiring information is a latent theory—a theory about the nature of information, the nature of the entities under study, the kinds of information that are valuable, and the proof structures that are acceptable. Research on individual differences, such as gender differences, for example, employs an ostensibly straightforward method. Participants are divided into the relevant categories (in this case, male and female), and then compared or contrasted on indices of the behavior or attribute under consideration. But many additional methodological choices and epistemological decisions lie outside the framework. Why is gender assumed to be a critical social category? Why are differences held to reveal more information than similarities? Are there in fact only two sexes, or is sex better represented as a continuum? How large a difference makes a difference? How are we to construe and evaluate the significance of the differences obtained? If women were to appear more passive than men, for example, do we say that women are overly passive or men are hyperactive? If women attend to more stimuli than men, do we say that women are field-dependent or are they more aware and vigilant?

More generally, science holds that the object of study is to uncover universal laws about the natural or the human world. Experimentation focuses on difference; nothing can be learned from similarities. Thus, an experiment that yields a finding of no difference—a failure to reject the null hypothesis—is considered one from which no conclusions can be drawn. Further, the particulars discovered are regarded as instances of general uniformities, uninfluenced by evaluative components in the scientist or the society. The methods of positivist research *decontextualize* the objects of inquiry, removing them from their everyday settings in order to isolate and identify certain aspects. They force complicated and rich experiences into mechanistic forms and orders. As Mary Parlee (in press) has observed, when psychological and social phenomena are reformulated in language that fits within the framework of positivism, they are "deformed" in various ways. In sum, the interest in prediction and control, and the search for formal laws and theories in psychology, is not so much wrong as limited. Positivist science can only play a secondary role in the task of interpreting life as a whole, including what has been submerged and avoided (Bredo & Feinberg, 1982).

The experiment, long the emblem of psychological research, has come under special scrutiny in this book. Reservations about experimentation have been registered at several levels. Rhoda Unger, for example, observes that traditional experimentation is designed to eliminate contextual influences on the behavior under study. Yet thoughts, values, and acts take their meaning from the social and political context that constitutes the individual. As Offred, the heroine of Margaret Atwood's *The Handmaid's Tale* (1986), says, "context is all." Rather than becoming detached from it, feminists are centrally committed to uncovering and analyzing that context (Dietz, 1987).

The overelaboration of methods and statistical procedures— the elevating of methods to methodology—has diverted attention from the processes of conceptual analysis, hypothesizing, and interpretation. "Doing psychology" has become equivalent to "doing experiments." But, the complex processes that lead to and define the experiments have been rendered invisible. Psychology, like any other discipline, entails a set of social arrangements. The experiment as a social situation provides the context that influences the behavior of its participants. The experimenter is not just an observer, but also a participant in the context created by the experimental proceedings. Several decades ago social psychology positioned the experimenter as a participant-observer in the research enterprise. But with increased emphasis on technology and methodology in psychology, the idea that the experimenter cannot be other than a participant as well as an observer has been put aside.

The emblematic status of the experiment leads us away from questions that cannot be studied by experimentation, dismissing knowledge gleaned by other methods as "not rigorous" or even "not psychology." This has led to the suppression of what Sandra Bem (1987) has called the romantic tradition in the behavioral sciences, the study of how the individual construes reality, "the content of the mind and/or the sociocultural processes that create that content" (257).

Some feminist psychologists have called for a shift from mechanistic experimental research to naturalistic studies, intensive interviewing, and participant observation. Thus far, however, these qualitative approaches have not been compelling to those working within American psychology's traditional paradigm because these approaches seem so readily influenced by the investigator's point of view. But if psychologists come to acknowledge that the investigator's subjectivity enters into *all* inquiry, including experimentation, then many objections to qualitative methods lose their sting. This recognition would encourage the acceptance of alternative methods of inquiry that view research not as detached but as engaged activity. This acknowledging of subjectivity would also underscore the importance of reflexivity, an awareness of the social bases of ideas and theories in psychology.

Gender and Knowing

Two divergent trends in Western thinking, each assumed by its adherents to be the right way to truth, have shaped the possibilities of knowing. The first is scientism, embodied in the positivist insistence on a rigid demarcation between observer and observed. Scientific detachment dictates that the observer be regarded as apart from the world under observation. Thus, the observer is removed from the world rather than situated at any point within it. The idea that the observer is not situated at any vantage point implies that he or she sees from all vantage points simultaneously. Similarly, the notion of objectivity implies that the observer's observations are not constrained by the sight lines of a particular vantage point.

The second trend is that associated with subjectivism. It asserts that the individual's knowledge of the world is direct, immediate, and prelinguistic, not involving interpretations or the constructions of science or common sense (Sass, 1988). In this view the self is seen as having a fixed and singular identity and as potentially being in touch with the essence of things. Such a self has the possibility of authentic self-knowledge, unimpaired by the customs and rigid habits of enculturation. This self represents the humanist ideal.

Although scientism and subjectivism have contradictory features, they have in common an underlying idealization of the individual. Both these ways of knowing imbue the knower with attributes of omnipresence and omniscience, attributes usually imputed only to the deity. Both positivism and humanism place the observer apart from the community of shared meanings and experiences. Such idealization of individual observers constrains their ability to reimagine gender.

CONSTRUCTIVISM AND GENDER

Constructivism holds that it is impossible to view the world objectively, without memory or desire. Our descriptions of the world provide information not only about the world, but also about ourselves as part of that world. Our theories and research tell us about ourselves. They furnish a map, not of the social world itself, but of the aspects of the social world that are deemed to deserve scientific attention and remain within our line of sight, our horizon. Thus Korzybski's (1958, 58) statement, "A map is not the territory." An example may make this clear. Considerable research has been directed toward answering the question of whether maternal employment outside the home is a threat to children's psychological welfare. But the question of how fathers' employment affects children has seldom been taken up. Similarly, the question of how maternal employment might *benefit* children's development receives slight attention. But even when a constructivist stance is deliberately assumed, the observer remains unaware of the light that illuminates the field, just as the fish is the last to discover the water. Reality as we perceive it and the category system by which we perceive it are, as Geertz (1984) puts it, "indissoluble." They cannot be separated.

Within a constructivist framework, the criterion for choosing between competing views is their utility. The question is not whether a particular view is correct or incorrect, an unanswerable question, but what the consequences of a particular view are.

Thus, the question is not "Which is right?" but "Which is best?" And the answer to the question "Which is best?" is another question: "Best for whom?" Because differing people have differing interests, the best view can never be determined absolutely. The focus of constructivism on utility and context suggests a connection between knowledge on the one hand and power and domination on the other. The Enlightenment idea that knowledge is emancipatory gives way before the contemporary recognition that knowledge is also, and perhaps primarily, a force of power and domination. In the extreme, such postmodern thinkers as Foucault view knowledge as a set of fictive accounts, endorsed by "experts," that establish and rationalize the power heirarchy. Knowledge is linked to systems of power that produce and sustain it, as many critiques of science and politics have shown. In turn, knowledge and meaning-making function to keep the power hierarchy intact.

Constructivism holds the promise of generating new knowledge about gender, but we must acknowledge that it also has limitations and even what some regard as dangers. The mechanistic nature of the language of some constructivists has been criticized as not capturing the richness of human experience. Some fear that the focus on meaning and language will turn feminists away from concern for the social, economic, and political problems associated with the material conditions of women's daily lives. We believe that a feminist constructivism can be crafted that will give a central place to women's lived experience.

The constructivist position within psychology is newly emergent and encompasses a variety of emphases. Indeed, as may be apparent, the constructionism of Rhoda Unger and the constructivism we describe are not entirely the same. Rhoda Unger emphasizes the individual as the active construer of his or her reality. We emphasize the ways an individual's reality is constituted through the discourses and practices of the culture. But as Laurie MacKinnon and Dusty Miller have pointed out, worldviews are constructed from both individual and collective vantage points (1987). What is important for feminists is how such worldviews reproduce and legitimize the subordination of women. As constructivist/constructionist approaches gain adherents in psychology, these and other points of disparity will be more fully aired.

POSTMODERNISM AND GENDER

Postmodernism allows us to express uncertainty about the grounding and methods for interpreting human experience. By opening up new ways of giving meaning to experience, postmodernism grants greater legitimacy to pluralities and diversities. Yet, some feminists advise against embracing postmodernism fully. They note that just when women and other excluded groups are finding their voice, postmodernism has declared voice an untenable concept (Hirshmann, 1988). Similarly, from a postmodern position, the concept of gender could be seen as merely a fictive account, and thus its value as an analytical tool dismissed (Alcoff, 1988). The invention of gender by feminists is the result of a lengthy struggle. Most are loathe to dislodge it from its position as a primary category of analysis, at least until its potential has been explored more fully.

Although we acknowledge the importance of these reservations, we take them as arguments for proceeding with caution, not as reasons for abandoning new initiatives entirely. In our view, a concern with meaning does not have to be dehumanizing, even though the abstract language of metatheory may have lost its referentiality. To assert that postmodern approaches are *the* correct way of viewing the world would violate the associated assumptions of postmodernism itself. Such an assertion would involve context stripping, holding that a single best approach existed for all questions, circumstances, and knowers. Indeed, postmodern strategies open possibilities by challenging dominant systems. Yet two critical questions face feminists interested in postmodernism. First, how can we embrace the relativism of postmodern thought without removing the intellectual grounds for feminist outrage over the treatment of women (cf. Hawkesworth, 1989)? Second, are there ways to retain the emphasis of American feminists on the material conditions of women's daily lives along with the postmodern focus on language and meaning? Such questions as these can help us ascertain the scope and limits of the territory of postmodern inquiry.

Conclusion

This book in no way completely describes feminist psychology. We have taken a bird's-eye view of the field, of necessity looking at major features of terrain and ignoring nuances and details. Sometimes we have found ourselves longing to agree with ideas we have critiqued. Just as many feminists call for an acceptance of diversity among women, we acknowledge the diversity among feminist theorists. Yet acknowledging diversity requires drawing distinctions, and for some, the drawing of distinctions will seem divisive. We have found in feminist psychology both alpha and beta bias, the exaggeration and minimizing of differences. We have questioned both scientism and subjectivism. We have challenged the positivist paradigm, which searches for one right answer. If diversity is to function as a resource for building new knowledge, we believe disparities must be acknowledged, perhaps even accentuated.

As we have explored questions of gender, it has become apparent that a tension exists between remaining grounded in gender and going beyond it. The study of gender in psychology has focused on ascertaining the attitudes and behaviors currently associated with women and men. One way of going beyond gender is to show that those attitudes and behaviors are not intrinsically connected to maleness and femaleness or even to masculinity and femininity. Rather, they are connected to men's and women's relative position in the power hierarchy or to their assigned roles in family life. So, for example, rather than studying women's speech, one might study the speech patterns of individuals in subordinate positions. Or, rather than studying women's morality or maternal thinking, one could study the ethos of care. Rather than debate whether or not the language of rights, autonomy, and personal freedom is male language, one could ask how such language is tied to power (Hirshmann, 1988). This is what we mean by "going beyond gender." A complete "degendering" of questions, however, would be a betrayal of history. Certain ideas, perspectives, and actions are historically associated with women (or men), and those associations are not merely coincidental but a product of social and material experiences. Thus, our inquiries need to be grounded in gender at the same time that they go beyond it.

The questions about the meaning of gender difference raised by the authors in this book lead to further questions. Can the question of the meaning of gender be answered? Should it be answered? A bad answer, as they say, spoils a good question. Even if gender differences could be identified, the *identification* of such differences would not constitute an *explanation* of those differences. In any case, the problems associated with establishing gender differences seem intractable. Rather than struggling in vain to dissolve uncertainty, we propose instead to acknowledge it and move beyond it. As John Dewey (1910) observed, intellectual progress usually occurs through the sheer abandonment of questions. We do not solve them: We get over them.

We end by recalling that theories persist as long as they are useful. Our examination of the meanings of difference in gender theory suggests that gender difference is no longer useful. Perhaps it is time to put aside difference and sameness, equal and opposite. Difference is, after all, only an aspect of sameness. The focus on difference, sameness, complementarity, and opposition has structured much of the psychology of gender. The answers are limited by the way in which the questions are posed.

We look to a paradigmatic shift that transcends dualisms of

mind and nature, freedom and determinism, individual and society, men and women. By recognizing that experience, purpose, and meaning are embedded in ongoing social relations,
feminist psychology has taken a crucial step toward this shift.
Feminist psychology can take a further step by recognizing how
our work practices, goals, and understandings are embedded in
the social relations of psychology itself. The disruption of old
categories and practices opens the way for new interpretations
and meanings.

REFERENCES

Alcoff, L. (1988). Cultural feminism versus poststructuralism: The
  identity crisis in feminist theory. *Signs, 13,* 405–36.
Atwood, M. (1986). *The handmaid's tale.* Boston: Houghton Mifflin.
Bem, S. L. (1987). Gender schema theory and the romantic tradition. In P.
  Shaver & C. Hendricks (Eds.), *Sex and gender* (251–71). Beverly Hills: Sage.
Bredo, E. & Feinberg, W. (Eds.). (1982). *Knowledge and values in social and
  educational research.* Philadelphia: Temple University Press.
Brown, L. S. (1989). New voices, new visions: Toward a lesbian/gay
  paradigm for psychology. *Psychology of Women Quarterly. 13,* 447–460.
Crawford, M., & Marecek, J. (1989). Feminist theory, feminist psychology:
  A bibliography of epistemology, critical analysis, and applications.
  Psychology of Women Quarterly, 13, 479–494.
Dewey, J. (1910). *The influence of Darwin on philosophy.* New York: Henry
  Holt.
Dietz, M. G. (1987). Context is all: Feminism and theories of citizenship.
  Daedalus, 116 (4), 1–24.
Flax, J. (1987). Postmodernism and gender relations in feminist theory.
  Signs, 12, 621–43.
Gadamer, H. G. (1976). *Philosophical hermeneutics.* Berkeley: University
  of California Press.
Geertz, C. (1984). "From the natives' point of view": On the nature of
  anthropological understanding. In R. A. Shweder & R. A. LeVine (Eds.),
  Culture theory: Essays on mind, self, and emotion (123–36).
  Cambridge: Cambridge University Press.
Gordon, L. (1988). *Heroes of their own lives: The politics and history of
  family violence.* New York: Penguin.

Handy, C. (1978). Going against the grain: Working couples and greedy occupations. In R. Rapoport & R. Rapoport (Eds.), *Working couples* (36–46). New York: Harper and Row.

Haraway, D. (1983). A manifesto for cyborgs: Science, technology, and socialist feminism in the 1980s. *Socialist Review, 80,* 65–107.

Haraway, D. (1989). *Primate visions: Gender, race, and nature in the world of modern science.* New York: Routledge.

Harding, S. (1986). *The science question in feminism.* Ithaca, NY: Cornell University Press.

Hare-Mustin, R. T. (1988). Family change and gender differences: Implications for theory and practice. *Family Relations, 37,* 36–41.

Hare-Mustin, R. T. & Marecek, J. (1986). Autonomy and gender: Some questions for therapists. *Psychotherapy, 23,* 205–12.

Hartsock, N. C. M. (1985). *Money, sex, and power: Toward a feminist historical materialism.* Boston: Northeastern University Press.

Hawkesworth, M. E. (1989). Knowers, knowing, known: Feminist theory and the claims of truth. *Signs, 14,* 533–57.

Hirshmann, N. (1988, 21 April): *Remarks on the meaning of difference.* Paper presented at the Penn Mid-Atlantic Seminar on Women in Society, Philadelphia.

Hollway, W. (1984). Gender difference and the production of subjectivity. In J. Henriques, W. Hollway, C. Urwin, C. Venn, & V. Walkerdine, (Eds.), *Changing the subject: Psychology, social regulation, and subjectivity.* (227–63). London: Routledge, Chapman & Hall.

Keller, E. F. (1985). *Reflections on gender and science.* New Haven: Yale University Press.

Keller, E. F. (1987). On the need to count past two in our thinking about gender and science. *New Ideas in Psychology, 5,* 275–87.

Korzybski, A. (1958). *Science and sanity* (4th ed.). Lakeville, CT: International Non-Aristotelian Library Publishing Co. (Distributed by the Institute of General Semantics.)

MacKinnon, L. K. & Miller, D. (1987). The new epistemology and the Milan approach: Feminism and sociopolitical considerations. *Journal of Marital and Family Therapy, 13,* 139–55.

Papanek, H. (1973). Men, women, and work: Reflections on the two-person career. *American Journal of Sociology, 78,* 852–72.

Parlee, M. B. (in press). Feminism and psychology. In S. R. Zalk and J. Gordon-Kelter (Eds.), *A revolution in knowledge: Feminism in the social sciences.* Boulder, CO: Westview Press.

Reinharz, S. (1985). Feminist distrust: Problems of context and content in sociological work. In D. N. Berg & K. K. Smith (Eds.), *Exploring clinical methods for social research* (153–72). Beverly Hills: Sage.

Rose, H. (1983). Hand, brain, and heart: A feminist epistemology for the natural sciences. *Signs, 9,* 73–90.

Sass, L. A. (1988). Humanism, hermeneutics, and the concept of the human subject. In S. B. Messer, L. A. Sass & R. L. Woolfolk (Eds.), *Hermeneutics and psychological theory* (222–71). New Brunswick: Rutgers University Press.

Smith, D. (1979). A sociology for women. In J. A. Sherman & E. T. Beck (Eds.), *The prism of sex: Essays in the sociology of knowledge* (135–87). Madison: University of Wisconsin Press.

Index